Intimate Antipathies

GIRAMONDO

Intimate Antipathies

Luke Carman

First published in 2019
from the Writing and Society Research Centre
at Western Sydney University
by the Giramondo Publishing Company
PO Box 752
Artarmon NSW 1570 Australia
www.giramondopublishing.com

Designed by Harry Williamson
Typeset by Andrew Davies
in 11.25/14 pt Garamond 3

Printed and bound by Ligare Book Printers
Distributed in Australia by NewSouth Books

A catalogue record for this
book is available from the
National Library of Australia

ISBN: 978-1-925818-12-3 (pbk)

9 8 7 6 5 4 3 2 1

For Leroy

That 'writers write' is meant to be self-evident. People like to say it. I find it is hardly ever true. Writers drink. Writers rant. Writers phone. Writers sleep. I have met very few writers who write at all.

RENATA ADLER, *Speedboat* (1976)

Contents

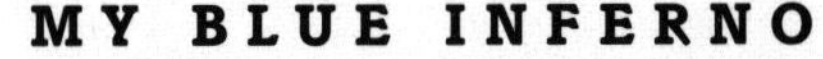

MY BLUE INFERNO

In the beginning I made the mistake of wanting to be what some people call a writer. This was a great disappointment to my father, who argued God had given him a handsome and well-formed child who ought to show his gratitude for those blessings by becoming a Kmart catalogue model. Many occasions were spent in my father's kitchen, each of us leaning against the sink, poring over the winter range of plaid vests and bomber jackets, and he would slap the pages and say, 'What did I tell you! This could have been you!' But it is the duty of every decent son to frustrate his father's wishes, and as art and literature seek to teach us, homeopathic parricide is the path to self-discovery.

Refusing to deal with the strange vanity of the life my father had picked out for me, I spent my time with books instead, in the dim light of my room, prone on the bed, eschewing all other dimensions of life, with its flashing passions and its baser seductions. I lived a life of ascetic unreality, all the while consoling myself for the wretchedness of my condition, with the sanctimonious air of a zealot, that my destiny was to be an inhabitant of the richer realms of the imaginative plains – and one day to be paid to write books in some squalid darkness, a room of my own and some fifty pounds – and to remain a stranger to the trappings the normies on the streets outside would never quit their fretting over.

Of course this was the fever dream of naïvety. The literary world, as it has been revealed to me in snatches at author panels, at lectures in university chambers, in conversation with poets in empty auditoriums, and while sitting quietly in psychiatrists' waiting rooms, is a public engagement, where the dim spotlight is always indifferently fixed, and the crowd around the gloom is made of pleasant faces and critics and other young writers who look on with a tame, cannibalistic attention. It's not so bad, not a heavy burden, but having met with some small success, I found I'd soon acquired all the trappings of a normal life: a wife, a home, a child, and an amount of respect, all of which I had not the faintest idea what to do with once they had come into being. Having failed at avoiding life and all its accessories, having discovered my dream of a wretched hermitude was an illusion, some lodestar of my mind decided it was time to collapse, and I found myself suffering from an active case of going nuts.

Having since recovered, after taking my pills and walking the line for a while, I went with my friend Tom to a café were poets were set to read, to celebrate being well again. People were knitting at tables in the dim candlelight, drinking wine and facing a microphone. I was drinking the wine in large gulps to avoid the taste, and several times before reaching my seat returned to the bar to have the glass refilled. I kept asking Tom if he could use another drink himself, but he was too busy fiddling with a packet of sugar and frowning at the poets on the stage, his red hair curled tight in the darkness.

'This poem is about softboys,' the short woman on stage, whose tattoo ran down her thigh like an oil slick into her socks, announced to the darkness. She began to read her softboy poem from a chapbook folded open in her hands, but the wine was making it hard to hear, and Tom was frowning so loudly, and my glass was empty.

At that moment, a great fat woman walking past the event with a lugubriously loose gait stopped before the glass of the café front and plonked her head against it, peering in at us and holding up her hands like fleshy apertures. Other people continued to pass her by on the street, but she stayed there, her plump hands up to the glass, her heavy breath casting a halo of fog around her face, as the poet, oblivious to this distracting inquisition, continued to deliver her delicate internal rhymes.

'Hey!' The big stranger's voice, booming through the glass cut across the poetry, 'What are you cunts doing?' she demanded. A nervous giggle wormed its way through the dark room. The short poet was turned almost in knots with her paper and legs and head in an array of directions, frozen in uncertainty. The large woman, her dignity hurt by the laughter, lifted up her top, and slammed her enormous breasts against the window, swirling them about in a windmill motion she had doubtless deployed in other such scenarios, as she screamed 'Get a load of these!' The atmosphere, as they say when a performance is elevated, was electric – no one dared to breathe lest they miss a moment – and as suddenly as it was done the woman bounced off the window and into the night, leaving a smear of circles behind, her great buttocks high and proud as she wrestled her showstoppers back under cover. With perfect timing, the audience still in their shock and awe, Fiona Wright, a famous poet who was sitting at a table in the back of the room, dropped the needle back into the event by calling out, 'and they say Newtown has gentrified!'

It's hard to say what it was exactly that caused it, but something about this commotion inspired Tom to leave without saying a word, his head probably strained by the effort of frowning. Eventually the man at the bar refused to serve me, so I left too. I caught the slow train back to the mountains on my own, watching the blurred shape of Sydney unwinding its high-rises, the lights on top of cranes like little fires on a distant hill, watching the legs of people at the stations flash in and out of the train at each stop, listening to kids talk their new codes for old things, the smell of grease and sweat and wine in the carriage, all the way up into the quiet, empty mountain air, where my breath trailed beyond me up the stairs of the station and onto the street. I needed to see if it was too late to get a beer at the pub, my blood was beginning to lose its drink, and that awful throb of sobriety was building in my temples.

The pub was dark, the lights were on in the car park but the doors were barred. A tall man in a black jacket appeared, charging towards me from around the other side of the street. 'Gimme your fucking wallet!' he demanded. I took a step back with my hands out in the international gesture for 'Oh!' He told me again to give up the wallet, and as he came closer I had nowhere to go but back onto the empty highway. I suppose I was thinking, 'He can't rob me on the road – it's too dangerous!', and for a moment this strategy seemed to work. He stopped at the edge of the gutter, his face contorted with rage and his shoulders flared. Then it occurred to me, strange to say, that he was hardly a man at all, probably just eighteen. I walked back towards the man in the jacket, his fearsome face still frozen into a mask of rage, but he retreated a few steps, as if he needed to maintain the distance between us. I started to laugh, and under an orange streetlight by the window of the bar I felt an enormous rush come into me. Through the throb in my temples and the last drop of drink in my blood and some reptilian part of the brain came some flux of spontaneous speech. I cursed him, belittled him, told him that he was the worst thief I'd ever met, mocked his stupid jacket and his soft face and his laughable attempts at robbery. He stepped backwards as if stunned, looked down at the ground for a moment, then sat down. He put his hands to his head and started to weep. I could not believe my eyes, the lad was crying in the gutter, but I could not restrain myself, or take pity on him – some wild power of words was erupting out of me into the night. I stood over him and put my face near his, and carried on ranting and raving. He was sobbing, and from my belly to my mouth there now came an electric current of abuse and sermonising that might have gone on forever had not a group of young men come running over from the pub car park and chased me away from the thief, thinking maybe that I must have attacked him. I walked away, and they did not chase, but stood around their new companion in a strange circle of confusion.

The words, however, would not cease, I walked home, become one of those people you sometimes hear passing your house in the dead of night, who are possessed by some spirit to rant and rave at the stars and the black trees moving in the midnight breeze over fences and the cars that go by. When I reached home, I stood at the doorway and went quiet. There was, I decided, finally nothing left to say. At that moment, an email appeared on my phone. It was from the editor of a long-standing literary journal. It read, 'I was wondering if you had any thoughts on the life of a writer?' As it happens, I did. I went inside, and began to write this odd book.

GETTING SQUARE IN A JERKING CIRCLE

When asked to explain why he had dedicated his long life to American letters, Gore Vidal hypothesised the existence of two distinct sub-genres of 'writer'. The first he described as operating in the Henry James caste: a writer obsessed – for no discernible reason – with perfecting the subtle arts of written language. Someone for whom, as James himself put it, 'there is only one recipe – to care a great deal for the cookery'. For these writers, their body of work represents an ongoing experiment with the vast frontiers of language. They live in search of the flawless scene, a numinous sentence – they wander intoxicated by belief in a transcendental sublimity obscured behind the dead space of everyday speech. Enquiring for motives from these linguistically possessed individuals is futile – they are as unable to reveal the source of the desire behind their odd impulses as the moth might be said to understand the allure of the flame.

The second category Vidal proposed was that of the unhappy soul who, at some pivotal point in their infancy, suffered psychic injury – an intolerable wounding of the self – for which the only remedy was the consoling prosthesis of imagination. Whatever enigmatic computational process in the human mind is charged with the interpretation of the world through language, in these benighted psychic cripples the system has been rerouted to conjure up alternate ontologies in which life's injustices can be undone, and remade. Such a crutch, Vidal suggested, becomes so necessary for the subject – and the processes involved so dominant – that the individual ultimately exists in a schismatic state between the unforgiving world of the real and the seductive realm of their own private fictions. To be so torn is to be a permanent émigré between states: to live an excess of lives, all of them in a kind of impoverished 'not quite' present. To experience the self as 'complex and many' is to be no one and nowhere in a sense; to reside in envious relation to the unity of the 'one and simple'. Those who inhabit the in-between world of their own imaginations typically make second-rate citizens in those unmalleable parameters we colloquially refer to as 'reality'. They lack the consistency, the focus and the commitment to thrive in most daylight vocations. The only suitable recourse open to such 'complicated' unfortunates is to scratch a living from exploiting their fantastical reflexes.

Having created this dichotomy of the two kinds of essential writers, Vidal placed himself squarely in the latter category. In his case, the reason for retreat into the imagination was an alcoholic mother. Like most of Vidal's commentary on matters literary, his psychoanalytic conception of a writerly split between the automaton nerd and the diseased dreamer is subtly honed to provoke derision from precisely the sort of literal-minded type who would ask an author such an imponderable question as 'why did you write?' in the first place – journalists, rationalists, theorists, pundits, pedants – those peers, in other words, who Vidal seemed to delight in antagonising. It hardly matters if the whole idea is a ponderous nonsense. As Alfred Whitehead recognised, it is more important that an idea be interesting than that it be true.

This essay – though you might not have guessed from its beginning – is an insider's account of the current state of Australia's so-called 'writing culture'. I begin with a long digression on Gore Vidal's ideas because I've always been struck by how strangely they fit the writing world as I've known it – and despite possessing nary the semblance of a profile myself, I tell you I've known it quite well. If nothing else, I have had the privilege of being in contact with countless young and 'emerging' writers over the last decade. For the last ten years I've run workshops and tutorials and projects and lectures in dozens of schools, universities and writing centres across the country, attempting to teach what little I know about the subject of literacy and literature to whomever is naïve enough to listen. Simultaneously, I've had the strange pleasure of being surrounded by some of our culture's most celebrated writers, critics and editors. It's not difficult to do so. The pond is small and the fish are big. Amidst the hopefuls I've taught, or the accomplished writers I've encountered, there is only a tiny fraction who might belong to Vidal's first category of the Jamesian word-nerd. From hopeful high-schoolers to venerated Miles Franklin clubbers – the overwhelming majority have been of the basket-case variety. Childhood traumas, mental illnesses, immutable shame, neuroses of every colour and shape, these are the ubiquitous hallmarks of the writer in persona. There have been perhaps one or two exceptions I've come across (both of them poets), who seemed more concerned with the shape of their sentences than making themselves whole – but that's it. If such an imbalance alone was not enough to suggest a flaw in Vidal's configuration, there is also the hollow ring of a bygone era in his distinctions.

I suspect a new subset of wounded-psyche-driven figures is in ascendance: those who – borrowing again from the categories above – appear to have dealt with their intolerable damage, not by indulging their creative faculties in the consolations of the imagination, but with fantasies of finding a home amidst those who do. Rather than retreating into the fecund vortex of other worlds and parallel realities, these dreamers conjure visions of themselves at play – accepted, affirmed, and celebrated – within a 'real-world' community that already exists: their great dream is to be welcomed into the bright and glimmering constellation of the Arts Industry. Crashing against the cruelty and capriciousness of the real, these types – while just as nutty as the poor writer-to-be who has a head full of linguistic ticks and slippages – imagine a kinder, better, softer arena of life awaits them in the open arms and exalted sentences of the arts community.

Of course, the writer-to-be and the arts community dreamer are not mutually excluded from being one and the same person, but when the latter does without the former, it becomes impossible to keep those who want to deal with words from colliding with those who'll do whatever it takes to 'make it' – and one is far better suited to the clash than the other. The advantage is almost always on the side of the cunning social arts satellite than the demented scribbler. In a culture like ours, one which places so little value on the linguistic traditions and our literary heritage – one in which the education system actively devalues it – those with relatively meagre talents and hopes of escaping into the safe spaces of the arts community often consider the 'writing' world as an easy option. Reality TV shows like *Australian Idol*, *X-Factor*, *The Voice* and so on have taught a generation of Australians that to be involved with music requires being humiliated and exposed for any delusions of talent they might have. Acting, likewise, is off-limits to the ugly and uncharismatic, so there are no chances there. The plastic arts require a modicum of ingenuity, the learning of a new and obtuse language, and an absurd level of tenacity, before one can even begin to bluff one's way into its clubhouse – all far too taxing. The writing world, as Henry James tells us, is a house of not one, but a million windows – and out of each pane stares a deranged shut-in whose fantasy novel about a dystopian post-apocalyptic planet enslaved by telekinetic Tuataras is a mere decade from being self-published online; or a poet who's just returned from summer in Berlin and is feverishly devising centos derived from official UN reports on Australia's asylum-seeker policies to be printed in the form of origami birds. These aspiring exiles are legion, and amongst their number are our nation's future paragons of poetry and prose. Not all of them will make it – exposure, if it comes, will kill more of them than it makes. Nevertheless, I have nothing but love in my heart for each and every one of our literary wannabes – I am one myself, after all, and will likely still be one when I'm laid in the dirt. The wannabe arts dreamers, on the other hand – desirous of making themselves part of this picture but indifferent to its meaning – observe the mosaic of tinkering revenants and their culturally irrelevant obsessions, and see an unguarded hen-house of nervous, leaderless fowls. They goose-step their way through the open borders of the writing culture with nothing on their minds but belonging. And why not? Perceiving themselves as creative, intuitive, passionate people inflamed with a sense of revolutionary zeal born from the resentment they carry in their hearts for those with genuine talent, these promising young things soon hold in their soft little hands the naked flesh of our nation's literary future.

Hearts a-flame with envy, bearing gifts of suppression, control, and a contagious spirit of nihilism, the social arts hopeful perceives themselves as an inherently creative djinn. Their existence is itself a miraculous creative act, and they secretly scorn those who bother to make things in earnest. Writers, in the minds of these 'change-makers' are block-headed toddlers playing in the sandbox of culture. The arts dreamer has larger game in their sights. Rather than fiddling about with the ephemera of fiction, they are busily revising cultural institutions; rather than piddle with obsolete publishing fancies like novels and the like, they are pulling the strings in funding decisions. Forget revolutions of thought and consciousness, these visionaries are drawing together the next generation of writers from the dust of our collective cultural vacuum! Given enough support, these 'king-creators' transcend the literary landscape, they become gods capable of making and unmaking from on high. As the cowardly writers of poetry and prose peek meekly out of their share-house windows between deleting and repeating their maggot-minded sentences or stanzas, those dreaming of positions on funding panels and advisory boards take up the call and make real, meaningful decisions about what will and will not be in our nation's literature. The problem is, these guardians of the culture view art as a means to power. In order to ensure their claims on their positions, they invariably screw down in the direction of a populist consensus within the arts community. They do so because they're political animals in a way that writers usually aren't. Artists are uncommonly indifferent to power, which is why they so often struggle to thrive without aid. The arts dreamer, a natural politician, lusts for the small power of the cultural now. They aren't necessarily powerful people – often all they possess is opinions – but opinion counts for a great deal when working with something as elusive as quality in the arts. Opinion, besides, can be traded for authority if one has an eye for cultural economies. In a few short years, with the right reparations, anyone without a shred of originality or integrity can be holding court, and dictating terms for an art form to which they contribute nothing but their lordly presence. The question of talent, of course, never comes into the opinion-shaper's equations. The general consensus of our culture is that there's no legitimate basis for determining the value of literary talent in the twenty-first century, so possessing it is superfluous – likely a hindrance, since it will probably make the rest of whichever literary clique one settles into suspicious of your wilfully un-egalitarian nature.

Much of the blame for creating the chasm in our culture from which these deluded demi-gods of arts management have risen must lie with the universities – and the corrupting influence of 'creative writing' courses which serve as cash cows for their beleaguered and fatigued humanities departments. A recent *Onion* article titled 'Creative Writing Professor Takes Time to Give Every Student Personalized False Hope' spread through the halls of my university. Its barb, obviously, was the betrayal of the young and wishful by the peddling of insincerities and fantasies under the banner of creative writing. Every student who sits in on a tutorial is encouraged to believe publication is only a degree away. It is a cruel lie, perpetuated by the complicity of tutors and lecturers who have no recourse but to toe the line. The directive to avoid the truth – formerly, I'm led to believe, of some concern to the humanities – is driven by the perpetual commandment from upper management to commericalise or perish. The arts and humanities might do well if only they would invert themselves and become something else. Enrolment numbers, meanwhile, are looking better than ever, and those hopeful students who just want to know how to get their novel or their poetry collection published continue to be seduced by a watered-down exposure to literary criticism, and kept slyly away from the reality that a high distinction in a creative writing course is no indication of – indeed, equally as likely to count against – their chances of ever being published. The average undergrad remains blissfully unaware that the slush piles of publishing houses groan with the weight of rejected submissions from creative writing lecturers. Many students, after being ushered through the most adequate training money can buy, have their first real-world encounter with the publishing industry when their doctorate-cum-fictionalised autobiography – a work they've spent ten years writing – is rejected by an intern who has happily never heard of René Girard's mimetic theory, or been interested in how the author has subverted the 'immolated victim' trope through an account of middle-class disorder in rural New South Wales. As an aside, it's astonishing how all the post-structuralist literary theory on earth suddenly seems like froth and fury when it crashes up against the stolid indifference of a rejection letter.

Little wonder then, in a sector of the arts populated by lunatic fantasists presided over by scholars enslaved to the demands of corporate universities, that the small masters of today who lust for power over the literary world are able to infiltrate our most sacred spaces completely unimpeded. And here I might as well drop all pretence – the social climbers of the arts – dragging their legions of Twitter followers behind them like some chain-link serpent's tail – are not merely ambitious arts workers: they are anti-artists in human form. They are incorrigible frauds and fakes. Since it will be called reactionary drivel to say so in the current climate, I might as well pre-empt accusations of Mark Latham-levels of bilious filibuster and borrow Holden Caulfield's refrain: these people are *phonies* – and our literary scene is corpulent with the weight of them.

Since it is all too easy to throw around the vague and self-serving assertion that there are vampires in our midst without offering any means by which to spot them, I offer this provisional guide for discriminating the fakes in our lit scene from the genuine article. Simultaneously freewheeling and coherent, the hucksters are nonchalant pundits on every cause and effect in politics and culture. They make wonderful guest spots on *Q&A*. They tread the boards of public spaces, making off-the-cuff speeches as effortlessly and gracefully as actors, and so they ought; though they lack the good genes to break into popular entertainment, they are born public relations agents for their own brands. Observe their capacity to charm crowds online and in-real-life without once stepping outside the bounds of accepted bourgeois-liberal consensus like angels twerking on a pin. Their every character trait, from mental illness to class background, is worn as an adornment of generic brand identity. Need an expert on the working class rural writer? They have one of those. Want someone to stand in as a borderline personality spokesperson? Speak to their agent. As the vibrant antithesis of the genuine, atrophied artist, they inhale and expand the increasing performativity of our literary culture with a gluttonous delight in their smiling eyes. Lastly, these devious characters can be identified by the breathtaking fervour with which they do nothing at all – and their insistence that anything they do not like is unmade. Only their own private vision of the world deserves life. Anything else is an abomination. Through the rigorous exercising of cultural opinion, they seek to decide who, what, where – and when – the flowers may grow in the garden. What they can't nip in the bud, they denounce as a weed in the blooming. To say these types hold nothing sacred is not to accuse them of being profane – they are merely quotidian proponents of a status quo that suits their slimy interests. To be subversive radicals would require them to believe in something other than themselves, and they do not – with the possible exception of their friends. What they mean by friendship is, however, some nightmarish Zuckerbergian conception of human connection. Their work, their brand, their audience, their reason for being. From the centre of their synapse-like social media webs, the vibrations of growth potential and social mobility are the only readings to which they are not completely numb. It would be one thing if these culture-creepers were merely usurping an unjust amount of the literary stage for themselves – after all, who *really* cares about the who's who of books? – but their repressive influence is one that poisons the lot of us – writer and reader alike. As the pall of their infiltration spreads over the nation, the atmosphere in the literary scene turns from disillusionment to despair. Speak to almost anyone in the fragile literary ecology: the spell of defeat is as thick as fog. This might seem hyperbolic, but the sheer magnitude of the malaise they have brought around our heads is a fatal one.

So then – having endured my jeremiad – you might well ask what proof I have that these malignants even exist. Admittedly, the evidence is difficult to produce. I don't have the nerve to name names, which would be the quickest way to make the case – but I can tell you where they are likely to live. It will come as no surprise that the largest infestation of these noxious weed-lingerers is to be found in the City of Literature itself – in a state with more literary festivals per capita than anywhere else on earth. This is not to suggest that every writer or writing organisation based in Victoria is the spawn of Satan – but Melbourne is known for proliferating mobsters, and its writing scene is no exception. The Melbourne literary mafia may have little 'real-world' potency, but that's not their game. Instead, they rely on an invidious power of suggestion that gnaws its way into the consciousness of young Australian writers. Their grim visage solidifies in the minds of our future writers, creating enough fog and smoke to overwhelm the victim and blind their common sense. In 'Right Time, Right Place: How the Melbourne Voice Shuts Writers Out', Jonno Revanche – an Adelaide-based writer – describes the internalised influence of the 'Melbourne Voice' on wannabe writers. Confronting the amassed cultural capital of the 'romanticised' City of Literature as a young outsider with aspirations of making it in the world of letters, Revanche describes a common feeling of despair: 'I would continually beat myself up over "not being contemporary enough", and felt like my honest words simply weren't valuable.'

Revanche's account of the Melbourne Voice's 'oppressive' influence paints this literary clique-hole as a cultish cabal holding the country's literary 'stakeholders' to ransom. It is an astonishingly implausible exaggeration of the power wielded by Melbourne's lit mobsters, but since it played directly to the vanity of these anti-artists, they were quick to laud Revanche's article as 'an important and necessary provocation' – the usual descriptor the clique-lords use to describe any opinion piece with which they agree. By contrast, Brigid Delaney's response piece in *The Guardian*, which suggested that the so-called 'Melbourne Voice' was a paper-thin mythological irrelevancy perpetuated by an insular crowd of insufferable literary-baristas, was dismissed by the anti-artists as a self-serving 'think piece' – the descriptor typically used to delegitimise any opinion piece with which the anti-artists and their disciples disagree. For what it's worth, there is, of course, no such thing as the 'Melbourne Voice', and the disenfranchising forces against which Revanche and Delaney are unwittingly united are the stateless anti-artists themselves. At the centre of the incestuous literary vortex – which outsiders such as Revanche and Delaney denounce with a kind of consoled envy – sit the anti-artists in residence, with their centrifugal charisma bending the world of Australian letters to suit their narcissistic whims. Though they have undoubtedly accumulated quite a presence in Melbourne – a particularly useful place to live if you have your heart set on squirming up the wobbly ladder of the community arts sector – their reach and their connections stretch beyond geographical borders.

James Tierney expressed the growing level of anxiety in the literary scene under the conspiratorial influence of our anti-artists in an article in *Kill Your Darlings* titled 'What Australian Literary Conversation?' Tierney characterises the titular conversation as 'one of long silences, punctuated by the occasional loud thud'. Contemplating the spasmodic silence of our critical dialogue, Tierney remarks: 'If there is a public literary conversation going it must be well hidden.' The kind of chatter about arts and culture that Tierney claims we ought to have a great deal more of is apparently exemplified by *Slate*'s popular 'Culture Gabfest' podcast. It's an interesting point – why can't we manage to be as open as our American friends? Why are we so intolerably shy whenever the conversation turns to culture? Perhaps unintentionally, Tierney provides an insight into the reason for our muted literary character when he considers Ben Etherington's combative 'Critic Watch' column in the *Sydney Review of Books*. Tierney praises Etherington's 'sharp gaze', one which – unlike much else that Australian literary criticism has to offer – managed to spark 'a lot of informal, private responses' within Tierney's hearing. It is apparently a rare thing that anyone in Tierney's earshot is roused by a bit of the old lit critique. Nevertheless, despite recognising Etherington as a decent critic who managed to stimulate at least *some* kind of literary chatter, Tierney feels compelled to share with us the 'concerns' he has 'heard' about Critic Watch, namely 'that it risks becoming a navel-gazing exercise – that to publicly and polemically consider the craft and broad judgment of Australia's critical culture could be both self-indulgent and self-regarding, the critical equivalent of a selfie.' Having slipped these concerns into print, Tierney then dismisses them as unpersuasive. There is, in this odd pulling of the punches thrown without any evident provocation, something bizarrely Australian. The critics assailed by Critic Watch are wrong, why worry about their anonymous misapprehensions – particularly if, as Tierney suggests, the whole thing is taking place in a vacuum of apparent indifference? Can it really be a coincidence that the only example of a critic who does what Tierney wants our critics to do is the one about whom he feels compelled to publish 'concerns' of 'self-regard'? When Tierney asks 'what conversation?' the answer is not the one taking place in print – it is the clandestine dialogue that is forever taking place on the periphery – real or imagined.

As a people, Australians are perhaps uniquely sensitive to the kind of censure that Tierney's projection establishes – it runs deep in our blood to be afraid of 'navel-gazing' and 'self-interest', derivations of the damning charge of being a wanker. Since Europeans stamped their dubious authority on its soil, this country has been an anxious, uncertain colony of a far-flung centre – and our literature (our literary condition) has reflected as much. Our predisposition towards an almost paranoid conservatism about arts and culture has perpetuated the idea that these things are inherently isolated from ordinary life, whatever that might be. Exclusive, repressive, and generally ashamed of itself, literature in this country has been shamefully abandoned to cultural guerrillas without a cause – who seek nothing but to further their interests even as they defuse the miasma of self-censorship and trepidation amongst our authors and readers as they ascend to power.

It's an old trick of the Australian cultural consciousness – every expression, no matter how legitimate, no matter how substantial, can be tossed to the winds by claiming that the person behind it has a hand down their pants. Our collective fear of our own awkwardness, our vestigial cringe at our own culture, is a powerful weapon in the anti-artist's arsenal.

The charge of wankerism was one that punctuated the climactic end point of a recent imbroglio over so-called 'middlebrow' literature. Ivor Indyk's editorial on literary prizes in the *Sydney Review of Books* kicked-off the controversy, arguing (with deliberate irony) that since the responsibility of discerning a prize-winner from any given sample of literary works is a duty too great to be entrusted to anybody at all, the money on offer might be better put to other uses. Hardly a contentious claim, and there might not have been any hand-wringing on the matter, had it not been for Indyk's embroiling of the middlebrow's influence into the mix. Indyk suggested that judges might be beholden to 'the whine of popular disappointment insinuating itself into their brains' when considering giving the nod to works that are 'challenging or innovative'. His 'target' was the nihilistic heckling from the peanut gallery – both real and imagined – which holds the language and imagination of a nation in a thrall of self-restraint.

Unsurprisingly, the prodding of this subterranean consciousness brought a slumbering neurosis roaring to the surface. But what turned the furore into a frenzy was a second 'middlebrow' piece published in the *Sydney Review of Books* by academic Beth Driscoll. Using novels by Susan Johnson, Antonia Hayes, and Stephanie Bishop as exemplars of the genre, Driscoll – author of *The New Literary Middlebrow: Tastemakers and Reading in the Twenty-First Century* – discussed the fluid and complex modes of literary appreciation that intersect the contentious terrain of the middlebrow. According to Driscoll, the works of these three authors offer readers, critics and publishers 'manifold pleasures'. Johnson, Hayes and Bishop did not take this compliment lying down. In their rejoinder the authors were 'as one in rejecting' the label of middlebrow – not to mention 'startled and offended' by Driscoll's 'collective dismissal of any discriminating powers of intellectual application to our respective works.' There's no act more gratifying an author can perform than sticking it to a critic – though this avenging trio demonstrates how much more satisfying it is to do so as a team – and the arguments Johnson, Hayes and Bishop make are persuasive. Hayes, for instance, points to Driscoll's 'vague definition of middlebrow', Bishop is concerned the piece 'unwittingly quarantines and belittles middle-class women writers, their books and a female readership', and Johnson – whose response is the least vexed of the three – just seems depressed by the whole affair.

The Melbourne-centred lit scene mobsters were quick to herald the responses of these writers as a watershed moment in Australian letters. Authors, this incident established, were now empowered to feel comfortable publicly refusing the 'pulling of rank' by righteous literary journals, critics, and academics – those institutionalised thugs who go about perpetuating hierarchical and ideological abuses against middle-class authors who just want to earn a crust in peace and in public. More troubling, however, was the emphasis placed by the anti-artists on a singularly polemical moment in Hayes' response. In praising Hayes' push-back against the *Sydney Review of Books*' 'war' on the middlebrow, the anti-artists chose to focus on her dismissal of the journal itself as one specialising in 'jerking off' (by way of reference to Susan Sontag). This kind of caustic accusation of 'wankery' amidst an otherwise measured response to genuine criticism plays directly into the hands of the anti-artists – it reinforces Tierney's observation that criticism and discussion surrounding literature is often de-legitimised by the accusation of being a giant wank. Literary culture, accusations of masturbation imply, should be driven by more meaningful, purposeful activity than shameful navel-gazing by critics and other unproductive members of society. After all, as Hayes asks, what are these 'diatribes' hoping to accomplish? The answer, of course, is nothing. It is the dogged moralising of the anti-artists that has perpetuated an ideology amidst our burgeoning writing culture that there is something other than an autotelic uselessness to be found in writing at all. Art, as the literary critic Terry Eagleton puts it, exists purely for its own self-delight. The anti-artists do their best to suppress this idea. In order to justify their positions on committees and in community groups and as festival directors, they need to create a powerful misconception that someone other than the artist is required to co-ordinate the manifest destiny of progress's perpetual march towards utopia through the alchemy of culture and industry.

It would be disingenuous in the extreme not to mention here that Hayes' final paragraph is one which draws me directly into the middlebrow debate. Accusing Luke Carman, Driscoll and Indyk of 'savage rhetoric', 'empty intellectualisation', ideological thinking, and 'jerking-off' (all things which I strenuously deny ever doing), Hayes asks, 'What are we supposed to do with these theoretical assessments? Indyk says awards are middlebrow, Carman says festivals are middlebrow and now Driscoll says novels are middlebrow.' Her reference to my view on literary festivals draws on a brief editorial I'd written for the journal some weeks earlier, and though it's true that the article wasn't exactly in praise of literary festivals, I didn't mention the term 'middlebrow' at all.

At the moment, as I type out the end of this rather odd essay, a violent storm descends on my home in the western suburbs of Sydney. Rain is spilling over the guttering, thunder shakes the floorboards under my feet and the ghost-gums spreading toward the city are roiling in heavy winds. It's an ominous scene and it fills me with a primal kind of dread. When I spoke to colleagues about the essay I was intending to write, they warned me that if I lashed out against the anti-artists in our midst, I'd bury my own career – I'd never, they said, be published by a literary journal in this country again. I'm not so sure about that. The massive cuts that have vivisected the literary sector have been devastating. It's not an optimistic time for those fighting it out in our literary coliseum – but there is a silver lining: the anti-artists have taken hits too. Right now, the gatekeepers are off their game, and there's never been a better time to burst out of their confines, and make your madding way in this strange world of lunatics, lovers and poets.

DIABOLUS IN FESTUM

This week, as the National Young Writers' Festival kicks off, and the Wheeler Centre announces the launch of yet another literary-themed festival, I am reminded of the enervating words of Gilles Deleuze:

> We sometimes congratulate writers, but they know they are far from having achieved their becoming, far from having attained the limit they set for themselves, which ceaselessly slips away from them. To write is to become something other than a writer.

Putting aside, for a moment, the begged question of what exactly the 'something other' is that one becomes when one writes, it strikes me that nowhere is Deleuze's complex of 'unbecoming' more evident than in the proliferation of the literary festival. It is, after all, the subtle duty of literary festivals and their variants to assure writers, with a vague but potent authority, that they are – despite their knowing self-doubts and anxieties – 'writers'.

Likewise, the audiences who fill the expectant rows of plastic chairs set out before ticketed, hour-long panel discussions on serious subjects such as 'Morality, Money, Entertainment and the Truth' and 'Is History Recoverable?' can assure themselves that they must be amongst that rarefied category of citizens who go by the epithet of 'reader', or at the least, consumers (and creators, why not) of some virtuous quantity called 'culture'.

If this sounds a little cynical, a tad polemical, then allow me to distract you with an anecdote. At a recent festival, after a pleasant panel discussion on 'How to Make It' between myself and three (much better known) writers, I was escorted to a signing table. Lacking both a pen to sign copies of my book, and people interested in possessing either my book or my signature, I was well placed to eavesdrop on a conversation between a Miles Franklin winner and an author short-listed for the Booker.

'That panel was all a bit of a wank, I'm not sure what the point was,' said the former.

'One might say the same of these festivals in general,' the latter replied.

At this point, the conversation ceased, as both men began to engage with their timid but slowly thronging fan-base. It struck me, as the queues to meet these quasi-celebrities accumulated before my eyes into an embarrassingly large number of people who didn't want to talk to me, that if two writers from the upper echelons of Australian letters were uncertain about the point of writers' festivals, then there was perhaps no clear and present point to such events at all. Which is not the same as saying that literary festivals are without purpose – were writers' and readers' festivals truly without a reason for being, they would have at least that in common with literature itself. But alas, as a shameless festival-hopper, I can attest that there is something suspiciously purposeful about your average literary 'festival'.

In my own, admittedly paranoid, view, festivals and their attendant events – though often advertised as opportunities for writers to connect and share their wisdom with their readers – are more akin to a form of trial in which the writer is put on stage to answer to the collective judgement of over-enthused readers. I mean no disrespect to those reading audiences – their hearts are in the right place – and they gaze up at the writers in front of them with affirming smiles and encouraging, almost knowing, expressions. But nonetheless, those hapless writers who do not conform to the conventions of this abrasive trial-by-sensibility are in for a gentle public shaming (on the level of a thorough skin cleansing) and will be 'daintily' ostracised from the festival circuit and thereby exiled – even if only by their own embarrassment – from an increasingly significant dimension of the writerly life. Thankfully, this happens rarely, as writers are preselected from the population to be the most malleable, passive and desperate-to-please people in the land. Despite the spinelessness of the writing demographic, so-called 'author talks', in my reading of them, are powerful affect-driven ceremonies (we laugh for those we love, cringe and fume at those we don't) that shape and reshape the writer according to the will of the market (which audiences have no choice but to stand in for at any given literary event).

The public performance of 'writer' that festivals and other literary occasions are set up to curate is an awkward amalgam of serious intellectual and clownish entertainer. Unfortunately, most book-makers – innocent vessels of linguistic reflex – are neither by nature.

Behind the curtains of the literary 'show', young writers are a-tremble with nerves as they whisper to the panel chair, 'It's my first time!' Luckily, a complete ineptitude for public performance (or even a total lack of character) is not as bad a handicap as the nervous young writer might believe: the dull medium of the panel discussion is its empty message. The curtain is pulled back, the young writer emerges into the glare of the spotlight and, after being asked about the origin of their debut work – a miracle: words, of varying degrees of coherence, flow forth. If the young writer pleases with her expulsions, then applause is sure to follow, and the transformation from scribbler to fully-fledged 'writer' is complete. The Emerging Writers' Festival is perhaps best up to facilitating this painful transformation, its very name promising a gentle progression into that definite form which festivals ask inchoate scribblers to assume.

Such public 'emergings' – or in the case of established writers, mutations – are framed as enriching 'cultural events'. This framing is somewhat suspect, but the way literary festivals typically describe themselves is outright duplicitous. One need only glance at the Sydney Writers' Festival's marketing to see that something doesn't add up. On the press image for a recent festival, we see someone lying in what appears to be a field of barley, holding up an open book in the late afternoon sun. If the image is meant to evoke Sydney, then it is a side of the city unfamiliar to me, and certainly nothing to do with Walsh Bay, where the festival was held. Then again, perhaps that's the point; reading is itself a kind of transportation, a movement between worlds. But that too is a problem, because the hands in the field belong to a reader, not a writer, and she is alone, as far from the festival as one needs to be in order to make the most of a book. In other words, the reader in the festival's own image is able to read because she has given the festival a miss. But perhaps I am being pedantic, and should leave the reader alone in her field; and I would, but hovering above her is the tagline for that year's Sydney Writers' Festival: 'It's thinking season.' What thinking has to do with the typical author talk or writers' panel is a mystery to me, and there – I know for sure – I am not alone. Even the SWF's hand-picked blogger, columnist and opinion-maker Benjamin Law, upon reviewing what he had learned from the festival in 2015, seemed only able to settle on the thought that he ought to be 'watching more TV'.

Perhaps I am looking at things the wrong way around. After all, despite what appears to be a lack of meatiness in the 'thinking' done on panels, it must be noted that Twitterers seem wholly committed to sending almost anything a writer has to offer into the eternal orbit of the digital ether, accompanied by epithets such as 'food for thought!' or '#insights'. There must, therefore, be something appealing enough in the rehearsed answers and well-practised performances that 'writers' meander through on panels to deserve reproduction *ad infinitum*. It is increasingly in the endless re-hashing of such speech-acts on the whirling gyre of Twitter that literary festivals live and die. After any given panel, one can observe writers furiously tapping at their Twitter feeds, searching vainly for something they said to have been selected for dissemination. The Digital Writers' Festival is perhaps the ultimate testament to this tendency for festivals to live on the internet, removing altogether the largely inconvenient and flabby necessity of festival venues, and running, instead, a series of online events that can be streamed live from writers' bedrooms and offices and directly into yours – whoever you are.

At this point I hear an internal critic accusing me of blatant disingenuousness. After all, won't I be knocking at the festival doors when they put out their calls? Won't I be down at the Wharf sipping champagne, nodding my head in some awkward encounter with someone I've never heard of as I stuff canapés into ziplock bags for my son's preschool lunches? Yes, indeed, I will. Come next year, I shall desperately await the invitations and the placements on panels – hopefully panels associated with a prize or two (another Premier's Award would be wonderful). For whatever horrors there are associated with the mechanisms of the literary festival, they have carved their diabolical mark upon me, and from that, there's no turning back.

A NORTHERN RIVERS ROMANCE

Tell all the truth but tell it slant –
Success in Circuit lies
Too bright for our infirm Delight
The Truth's superb surprise
As Lightning to the Children eased
With explanation kind
The Truth must dazzle gradually
Or every man be blind –

EMILY DICKINSON

It was an email from Alice, the editor at my publisher's office just up the hall from my own shabby desk that led me back to Byron Bay. Alice wrote: 'Well, you tried to get out of the festival circuit but they want you anyway.' Attached was an invitation signed by the director of the Byron Bay Writers Festival. Her letter read: 'It gives me great pleasure to invite you to participate in our 2016 program. For the last two years we have had some extra funding to run a "5 writers" regional tour in the lead up to the main festival. We put 5 writers in a van and send them to 5 regional towns in the Northern Rivers in 5 days.' Reading that first cordial offering – innocent as it sounds reproduced here – I saw the makings of a trap. It is difficult for me to explain the process that led to this suspicion, so I will stick to the associations and abstractions that occurred as I imagined what attending this affair might entail.

Admittedly, from a distance, to anyone unfamiliar with

the inside baseball of the writing world, the opportunity to be flown, feted and paid to partake in a festival on the north coast of New South Wales might sound like a gift horse, so to speak – but there was doubt in my heart. For one thing, the timing was dubious: the email in question had arrived in the aftermath of an editorial I'd written on the devilish nature of the writing culture, with particular contempt for the hubbub of festivals and their sinister rituals. Power-players in the so-called 'scene' had come to my little office in Bankstown to assure me that blacklistings had been put in place to keep precisely these kind of offers and invites to me permanently off the table. Were these power-players mistaken? They'd seemed so self-assured. To make matters more suspect, there was the fact that I had no new book to shill, my own slim square volume having long ago exhausted whatever modest readership it had managed to propagate. There was something in Alice's tone, too, that struck me as a clear and present warning – a subtle, but unmistakably imploring note of concern. Perhaps it was just her way of implying that I should not screw things up further than I already had with the industry; that I should make some friends for a change and stay off whatever high horse I might be tempted to ride. But one can never be too careful when reading between the lines. The sort of thoughts I'm describing here are paranoid fantasies. If I could have seen that at the time, sitting at my desk deliberating on the offer as the little delusions began to sprout, it might not have made much difference.

To weed out what was at stake in the director's invitation, I began to imagine the landscape of Byron Bay, so as to rehearse in advance the pitfalls awaiting. For a setting: the vague image of a beach somewhere: a bright sun and a long curving beach populated by tourists in shorts and thongs, the air stinking of seaweed and sunscreen, a hot burning sensation spread across my cheeks, and sand between my toes. High to the right, I saw a limestone lighthouse on a hill, and seagulls rising to a background of clouds. This seemed a suitable conception of a beachside *paradiso*, one likely to fit some part of the bay's picture. A memory intervened in this idyll: I remembered what it should not be possible to forget: for a while, at least, I was a married man, and had honeymooned deep in the forests of the riverlands of northern New South Wales, stopping and staying in Byron on the way there. Memories of our drive along the eastern coast of the country, as they reoccurred to me, and as I replay them again now, seem so estranged as to be the makings of a dream. The actors in these scenes look unfamiliar – they move in a watery motion that does not conform to the wooden clumsiness of recent years, their details are half hidden in the gaps and shade. Is it nostalgia that makes them look so nimble, and light – or some other error of translation?

In was in this dreamy unreality of the past that my wife and I stayed in a treetop cabin resort off a dirt track which wound between the forests of Mullumbimby, with the sounds of strange birds rousing us in the morning and a fine gold light glowing in the room above the bed. An alternative version of myself pulls back the blinds on the way to the bathroom, half-dressed, and sits on the cold slate toilet across from tall glass walls open to the dense forest outside the cabin. This stranger appears, in my recollections, to be watching the high-topped trees flicker in a green and gold sweat while rare feathers sweep between their branches, knocking seedpods through the long leaves. It is impossible to intuit what this thin young man is thinking. His hair looks great, or at least there is more of it. When night comes, armed with flimsy eco-friendly torches, and by careful footsteps on mossy rock, the couple creep to a shallow riverbed splattered with the iridescent oozing of a glow-worm colony clinging to the earth above the water. The wife, her long hair invisible in the dark, smiles to discover that her thin husband believes the worms to be living creatures. 'Just a conspiracy of impressions,' she says to the stranger, in a voice swallowed up by the damp echoing forest.

The moon comes out loud above them and the wife strips down to climb out onto a fallen tree bridging the riverbanks. He cautions her not to go out so far above the water, but she laughs and her skin in the pale light looks a mirage in the night-woods. It is perhaps because of the illusions of body and landscape that he does not react when the log first shakes and twists under her weight. The image of her out on the dead tree, naked as a forest nymph, with her strong hands holding her high above the flowing waters as she slides along the grainy length between the banks forces me, at this moment, watching and recalling the pair as they play their game by the river, to wonder if there is any truth at all to this series of recollections. Who was this thin man and his Lady of Shalott?

The body forgets itself in a rather final way: most nights, the world is very quiet, and the bed feels to my ever-thickening body like an examination table for the gods. Books pile up on the bedside, but there is nothing much to be found in those: more strangers in the sunken carriage. The doubt of memory runs so deep that I am compelled into the dark side of this room I am writing in to look through the drawer by the bed and find, sandwiched by a court summons and speeding fine, a little black case containing a wedding band. I am required to run my finger inside the rim, to feel the inscription which reads '*Ma armastan sind*'. It means 'I love you' in a rare antipodean language. The words, etched in white gold, help to hold the disparate dimensions of memory together. But the ring must go back to its tiny leather snare, and I have stepped away from the bed. Certainty climbs into a bed of fog and fades under its covers. Who is it, after all, at this table in a room in a house on a hill – who is it taking this strange tone of voice, who goes about believing the inscriptions inside a ring, or the impressions of images all lined up in a row like a stitching of feathers in the Mycenaean crown on the dry skull of an old chieftain, alone in his honeycomb tomb. For what it is worth: I recall that my new wife screamed when she fell into the river, and her knees were bleeding when we limped back to the room to pull the leeches from her wet body, with mud and blood on the bedsheets that night of our honeymoon.

I googled the five writers listed in the email in order to discern what it might look like to be trapped in the cramped confines of a rental with them for five days, and in doing so discovered a dispiritingly pleasant array of faces. Gabbie, Miles, Jesse, Zach, Kate: looking at their cherubic smiles and happy eyes, it occurred to me as I sat at my dishevelled desk in Bankstown that I could not have concocted a less compatible collection of fellow artists if asked to hand-pick them from an industry line-up.

The first potential van-mate I investigated was Gabbie Stroud: self-described as a 'lapsed teacher', Gabbie was easy to track down, a plethora of articles having only recently been written in praise of her essay 'Teaching Australia: Fight or Flight', which detailed the traumatic effects of an education system in crisis. The media consensus painted Gabbie as a courageous hero, speaking out with skin in the game, but I had my suspicions. Despite media support for her efforts, or perhaps because of it, I didn't trust some feature of her beaming smile, and the erratic curl of her hair in images online made me nod my head as though a dark flaw had been uncovered.

Miles Merrill, the second writer I studied, seemed even less commendable. A Chicago-born 'tour de force' performance poet, Merril's claim to eternity – the thing for which he will no doubt be included in all the history books of Australian literature in the twenty-first century (supposing any are written) – was having single-handedly transplanted the proud American tradition of poetry slamming to our southern shores. For that alone I figured he had a great deal to answer for, since poetry slamming, I considered, smug in my office in the western suburbs of Sydney, is a literary strain of cultural disease without redemption: a derivative, unlettered, poetaster's impression of art.

The novelist Zacharey Jane, a young-adult author with picture books about a willowy slumber-jack called 'Tobias Blow', was to be our tour guide on the road. To her name was also a novel, *The Lifeboat*, no doubt an artistic response to the 'children overboard' horrors of the Howard era. Accompanying these accomplishments was a distinguished career in the film industry – Zacharey had apparently not only met George Lucas, but designed light sabres for the much-maligned Star Wars prequels. If these things were not evidence enough of villainy, then there was the issue of her looks: rather too blonde and potently cheek-boned for me as I sat there glowering into the laptop screen.

Jesse Blackadder, meanwhile, who specialised in 'landscapes, adventurous women and very cold places', was another writer of children's books about mythical brumbies and Antarctic dogs. Her latest adult novel was set in the open sea with an eye on whaling in the 1930s. Jesse, like all the other writers assigned to the van, had the smiling face and bright eyes of people who have lived lives punctuated by joy, love, sadness and enthusiasm in ordinary measure, a look I considered, sitting at my desk, to be other than the ideal form the writer's visage ought to take. Somewhere in my decades-long study of the literary arts, I had come to believe, in my secret heart of hearts, that the author ought to be, in person, a vision of wrack and ruin – with a face as flat and deflated as an old leather-bound book kept in a cellar, the nerves in cheeks and forehead atrophied by long states of abstraction, the muscles of human expression never having been needed on what Jacques Derrida calls the long march into the world of dead, 'returning with bloodshot eyes and bleeding ears'.

At my desk in Bankstown, as I considered these faces, I saw a copy of Gerald Murnane's *A History of Books*, his perfect writer's face on the cover: a doleful lack of liveliness to his countenance, grim and fully deflated. Googling Gabbie, Miles, Jesse and Zach had revealed these potential road-tripper colleagues to be far from the morose Murnane ideal – but Kate Forsyth, the final van-mate, turned out to be its very antithesis. Not merely an unabashed writer of historical fictions with fairy-tale roots, the sort of writer who no doubt meets her characters in dreams and considers these collisions part of the profound mystery of fiction's magic, but a woman with luxurious raven hair framing an almost elfin face with loud dark eyes and a smile as might suit the characters in one of her enchanted stories. She was a writer, to my mind, unthinkably opposed to the deranged figure of the artist who must grapple with the entanglements of words between worlds, and the supreme enigmas of literature.

Upon the landscapes that had already been summoned up by the email – the white-gold beach with surfers and sunbathers, the frothing blue immensity, the fervid roads between the towns and rivers and bays, on which my wife and I had so long ago honeymooned – I projected a van full of the faces I'd found on the web, and amongst them placed an avatar of myself: seatbelt tight around the shoulders, the smiling faces of the other writers in their open intercourse, trying, occasionally, to bring me into their conversations with sympathetic looks and doubtful glances of pity when I seemed unable to return to them a signifier of relationship. The luggage crowded into the back of the van would be rocking and vibrating, the road rolling backwards in a nauseating spillage between the masses of gum trees glowing to a sunset filament. We unload at community halls in empty coastal towns, where gatherings of elderly readers sit plangent in plastic chairs, patient with our ramblings then thronged around book-signing tables after the applause, buying books and insinuating their own talents to us. I project those expectant faces and guide them into familiar foreign rooms, seat them, make them smile and stare. They are almost real, an imaginary audience with slumped shoulders in rows before an aching stage. I think, unfairly, of Patrick White's curmudgeonly face, and his line in *Voss*, 'All human relations are a lunge, the direction of which seems inevitable', and as I breathe out a highway of these thoughts, it feels as though the road and its memories have already been paved by them.

What I cannot see, what it is impossible for me to know, sitting at my desk in my office in Bankstown, dreaming of strangers and the distance between towns in the Northern Rivers, is the look of recognition that will cross Gabbie Stroud's face some months from now on the rattling shuttle bus taking us both out to the plane to fly north from Sydney. She is sitting at the back of the bus, and I am standing by a pole with one foot on my carry-on. Do I mouth hello or merely nod and smile? We lose each other in the crowd alighting the plane, but I see Kate Forsyth up ahead, her raven hair and full red lips like any prince's debutante in her lordly novels. Watching her toss the luggage overhead, I will hear Murnane's syllogism about two distinct types of writer – those fanciful kinds who make imaginary scripts for the reader's delight, and those who deal with the universal mind for the sake of an autotelic truth – reverberating in my mind like a mantra, but when the six of us meet at the airport in Coffs Harbour, corralled around our wheeled suitcases, shaking hands and asking how the flight felt for each other, the mantra will begin to lose its frequency. At a café close by, Kate will reveal a small chest of trinkets – crow claws, meteorite rings, jewels from distant places made from the tiny bones of extinct animals. A cappuccino warms my nervous hands and Jesse Blackadder talks to us about her latest novel while the sound of cups clink by the counter and three men in hi-vis stare quietly out the window. My inner monologue whispers a few lines of Murnane's that I'd committed to memory to keep me secure on the road with strangers, a long way from the consolatory estrangements of lofty words, frozen safely on pages in books:

In earlier years, I had used makeshift terms such as film-script fiction on the one hand and meditative fiction or true fiction on the other hand whenever I had tried to point out the differences between the sort of writing meant to bring to the reader's mind events such as might be witnessed in the place we call the real world and the sort of writing meant to disclose to the reader some of the memories or reflections or imaginings of the narrator of the fiction.

The current of those lines lifted the burden from space and time in the café, as if all my little sins might be abstractions, and all the slips and stumbling to come only a kind of dance. Not long after, hearing Miles and Gabbie talk about their lives, I say to Kate as if talking to everyone, 'To be honest, I am not sure what we do has any kind of meaning at all.' To which, tilting a pot to fill her cup, she says in a sweet lilting tone without taking her eyes off the pouring tea, 'Oh darling, but of course it does.'

All of this, though written in the chalked stone of the present as I sit at this computer in the dark and write these lines, was beyond me as I sat at the desk in my office and played with numb projections in the dread anticipation of the Byron Bay experience to come. Running the possible contours of the trip through my head as though the world itself were a mere simulation, proliferated by the idiosyncrasies peculiar to the conscious subject, I could not hope to image the look of delight on Gabbie's face when we walk into the lobby of our resort in Coffs Harbour, dragging our luggage behind us like monks devoted to luxury. It will make us all laugh quietly to see her wide-eyed wonder at the palatial glimmer of the marble slate floor and the wide expanse of windows open to the crashing ocean views and a fountain bubbling in the centre of the lobby which takes the form of a peacock's fan. She will communicate with her eyes that she cannot fathom what it is we have done to deserve such rich treatment: my inner monologue slowly ceases its whispering – though I am far from noticing its absence as we file into our rooms.

Gabbie and I walk at dusk through the hotel grounds, her curled hair glowing red at sunset. We emerge from a border of shrubs at the edge of the hotel's garden, and step through a static field of sandflies and out onto the talc-soft sands. Gabbie laughs the flies away from her face, and then we find ourselves between the waves and a lagoon lying still behind the dunes. Lost completely in the present, like a child, I throw a series of stones across the water and the gold light catches in their locutions. 'Not great at that, are you?' Gabbie says, and we agree to walk along the beach again in the morning and take photographs of the sunrise over the cliffs surrounding the resort. It will be late that night, when I sit in the heavy armchair by the hotel bar, with a champagne flute and tired eyes, that Zacharey, our blonde-haired tour guide, will say to me, 'Shut your mouth, you!' when I begin to discuss the troubles of literature. I tell Kate, 'There is no way to know what good, if any, fiction does for anyone at all, and all this talk about generating empathy is an ideological act of wishful thinking.' Kate, listening intently but smiling, says, with the dim lights of the bar still shining on her porcelain skin, 'I promise you, by the end of the tour I will change your mind.' I laugh, but the inner voice is quiet, and there is a vast silence in the room, as if a spell has been cast, and I say, 'We shall see', but do not hear the words. Kate will end the conversation with one last recitation from her story of the Succession of Kings – this time the tale of Charles II. She begins, 'This is the story of the king who ran.'

If I could see – sitting at my dismal desk in the western suburbs, with a heart beating erratic for the suburban world around me – the recitation in the hotel bar coming towards me from the Byron Bay tour, I would have declined, I am sure of it, if only, perhaps, because change is a frightening habit. But if I had not gone north, if I had stayed at the desk in Bankstown, I would never have walked into a classroom with Miles Merrill, and seen the subtle hysteria of the boys and girls in uniform as Miles stands before them in his full height, long-limbed and moving as if some infernal ecstasy has touched his blood; and I would never have noticed the looks on the two boys' faces, who turn to each other and ask 'What is happening?' as Miles begins his poem about a night camped out in the riverlands with storms passing over the trembling skin of his tent. I will see this, and watching closely, observe a subtle electrical storm rising up from the carpet around the feet of the students, bringing with it an eerie charge that pulses through the bodies of the children while the green of Ballina seems to glow brighter and louder out the classroom window. I am almost able to see the synaptic charge generated on the young faces as he performs the popping of rain drops on a tent at night that leaves the air without breath around us, and the sheer amazement on the English teacher's face as he shakes Miles' hand and thanks him for giving his kids such an unfamiliar gift.

This strange experience will stay with me, and later, when I ask about the electricity I saw seeping into the room when we are both back at the hotel and the sun has long since set, Miles will tell me that when he sits to write his poems, he feels a force of energy flow into the top of his head from some unknown dimension, and in the act of recitation, an equal and opposite energy comes up through the floorboards from the earth and enters his body, spreads out through his fingertips and into the atmosphere of the room. He says this to me and I strain hard to hear him over the rockabilly band playing in the bar, and just as he arches a finger to emphasise the magic, a drunken bridesmaid collapses around his neck and says, 'Can I please touch your hair? I've never seen hair like that around here!' I see a sorrowful look of resignation enter his eyes. Simultaneously, on the far side of the bar, Jesse invites us to have dinner at her home. If I had not been there to go along, on the snaking drive away from our hotel to Jesse's house, I would never have seen the storm-slashed bunches of banana trees by the waterhole of her property, and the shadowy shape of sacred mountains stacked on the night's horizon. In her dining room, surrounded by half the books ever written, Jesse shows me slides of adventures in the Antarctic – a white immensity beneath an endless sky punctured by the mirage of lightning-blue glaciers as large as cities, and bearded men with icicles clinging to their determined faces, and while I wonder at her private world, our tour guide Zacharey practises an elevator pitch for her latest novel before Miles and Kate, whose advice seems to have no limitations, and rolls on in laughter and nods of approval.

The next night, under a golden chandelier in a Coffs Harbour restaurant, Kate, with another glass in her hand and the endless stream of bubbles rising between her fingers, will say to me like an apparition from a cinematic dream, 'Sometimes a person will come into your life and give to you precisely what it is that you need to hear, exactly when you need to hear it.' I will reply to her, with the bell toll of the flutes between us across the round table, 'But I don't believe in gurus.' The inner monologue will know this is a lie. With bookshelves at our backs and white-haired readers thronged around us at a long set of tables with our respective books standing at attention, Kate rises like a siren to tell the story of her face. A dog savaged her when she was just a child. So badly did the animal make a mess of young Kate Forsyth, the doctors had to remake her. 'I was the first person in Australia,' she tells the crowd in her casual serenity, 'to have an artificial tear duct inserted.' In the time of her rejuvenation, tied to a hospital bed in a wrapping of fevers and blankets, she held on tight to the story of Rapunzel – from a book given by her mother – and the strange tale of the long-locked girl trapped in her tiny tower revolved obsessively through her consciousness as the doctors and nurses made their rounds and her torn face remade itself. I realise, listening to this story, as facile as it sounds to offer it here, as though all I am is the awed provincial walking through the gates of an ancient city, how feeble all my ideas have been to leave no room for all these other readers who have made sense of themselves and their place in the world through the messiness of words and stories re-remembered in their bedrooms and hospital beds and daydreams by the fire. There is, I saw in the embrace of the white-haired crowd and the sun-slicked Coffs Harbour street glowing at us through the window, a deep force in the workings of words that all my useless philosophising had left out altogether. Jesse warns me, as I confide some of this to her on the walk back to the van, the crowd walking with us, that I am coming under the spell of a master storyteller.

I watch these writers perform themselves night after night, hear their tales and bear witness to their stories of bookish life. At last, in a burlesque theatre in Brunswick Heads, with purple walls and abstractions hanged from the ceiling, Kate will ask me to take the stage with her, to play a role in one of her stories. She rewrites the scene to suit me, taking out the complicated words and all the French. It is a scene from her massively successful novel *Bitter Greens*. She wants me to play the role of the Marquis, to seduce her on the stage for everyone to see. 'I'll help you out,' she says. 'I'll fill you full of Veuve Clicquot,' and by the time it comes to stand before a full house of faces half-obscured by the bright lights angled at the stage, there are four empty bottles of champagne by our feet. Kate stands close to me and after we play out our game of chance on stage I say, 'I don't think I can resist you. I've never met a girl like you.' She says, 'I'm not that unusual.' I reach out for one more kiss, and she says, 'You've already taken more than we ever wagered!' I look into her eyes and say in a voice I didn't know I had, 'You will not be so cruel, Charlotte-Rose!' The crowd, when the debt is paid, cheers and claps and we toss our scripts into the dark behind the curtain. I realise, glancing at her red-lipped smile in the stage lights, remembering all my old maxims about the nexus of art, truth and fiction, that I've been set free from a naïve web of illusions.

On the final day of the tour we reach the festival proper. In a clubhouse on the opening night the managing director cries into the microphone when he thinks of the love and faith the volunteers have shown over the twenty years he has been in charge. At a panel in an enormous tent on a rainy day with muddied footprints smothering everything in sight, Gabbie makes an audience of hundreds break into tears and applause when she shares her heartache at having to give away teaching, and the students she so dearly loves. Zacharey chairs our final panel together, asks us to reflect on the experiences of the tour. In the crowd, three rows from the marquee door, I notice my book editor, Alice, and I cannot wait to tell her, through the microphone that is going to be passed into my hands, how profoundly this trip has changed my life. I will say, 'I know how trite this will all sound' – but before the microphone comes to my hand she glances at her watch, rises from her seat and walks out of the tent, her long black coat clutched tight against the rain.

Of course, all spells are temporary, though they may come back from time to time. What I couldn't know, sitting at my desk and wondering if I should take one path or another, or in my seat on the stage at Byron Bay, watching people come and go as we talk to them about how strange it was to feel so much for each other in our rental van, is that eventually a new present will arrive in time, and I will sit at a screen with these impressions and images moving through me like a series of dreams – not quite sure how much of it can be salvaged from the past, how much to leave behind, and how to alight the ride at some final, permanent stop.

On the long road north my wife and I parked in the shade between two cafés on a wide street in Bellingen, with purple banners staked beneath an enormous oak tree, to spray 'Just Married' on the back windscreen of our Holden with a can of shaving cream. Two hippies and a limp dog, the latter anchored to an awning post, watched us, and I shrugged my shoulders at them all to apologise for advertising the institution of marriage in their bohemian grove. The dog put its calico head to its bowl and shut its tired eyes. The sun was saturating. We'd had a few drinks at a pub on the highway, where I came upon a book of old photographs tucked into a wire stand on an empty window sill, and I flipped open to the image of a broad-shouldered man in thick boots and a heavy coat standing beside a foal-thin lad that we took to be an apprentice. Both men were looking up into the camera from inside a deep pit, and the bigger man's thick hands were wrapped solidly around a sledge hammer dripping with gore. Pig's blood covered the apprentice's white overalls, and was smeared across the curved walls of the pit. We put the book away and drank in the sun.

So grim, sometimes, the melancholia of all these images. I get up and leave the essay for a final time, check the pile of books beside the bed. Just inside the covers of *Bitter Greens*, I run my hands over the inscription inked inside that reads, 'May the Marquis live in your heart forever!' For a while I am back in Byron Bay, in the wet tents and the muddy fields, the treetop resorts and the luggage-heavy van, by the river with the worms, under the strange charms of a Northern Rivers romance.

AN INTIMATE ANTIPATHY

When I was a married man with all the usual pathologies of my time and place, I lived in a converted bakery on a street in St Peters where for some nights each year a vagrant would settle his body on the sidewalk outside our house. I'd see him in the surrounding suburbs when he wasn't camped on his bundles under our window, wandering by the Princes Highway some nights, or near the Officeworks driveway in Petersham, with his swollen trousers and blackened toes, and so I figured he travelled from point to point by some strange nomadic rhythm, coming back like the flowers on the jacarandas via a springtime of his own arithmetic. Often times there was so much dried vomit and spittle congealed in his beard that the drooping knots of hair looked like tree roots growing out from the cracks spread across his sun-ravaged face. The top of his skull was scalped red and white with welts and blistering burns from the long disassociated meditations he made sitting in direct sunlight by the roadside, hunched and motionless as an ancient ascetic petrified in prayer.

Though he never caused me any harm, I sure didn't like him hanging around. My wife would sometimes claim to have given him a drink of water or a piece of fruit, and once I thought I heard her asking him if he fancied an apple or a glass of milk while I was asleep upstairs. When made aware of my wife's charities I'd make my disapproval known, and ask her to leave the man to his own deranged devices, worried that by her influence he'd become like a stray cat that has reckoned on a reliable source of nourishment, and is forever afterwards pawing around the doorway for scraps of feed or some other attention. Worse still, though they say there's no link between deranged folk and violent crimes, I feared that he'd lock his whirling mind on my wife, on account of her kindness, and concoct a fever-dreamed reason for doing her harm. It didn't matter, my wife never listened to me about him or any other thing, and took my fears about the man camped under the window as the logical extension of her husband's fearful temper, prone as I was to paranoias and needless fretting. The more I pressed these concerns the more she responded with an expression which, though ostensibly blank, expressed through some subtlety an air of patient exasperation. I admit, too, to being disturbed by the low cries he used to make at night when what I took to be delusional fits of schizophrenia would transport him into an inner world of his own private imagining. Some nights, when sleep would not come, I'd sit in the dark of our bedroom, on a wicker chair by the window, listening to his cries. They put me in mind of the ejaculations a yelping animal caught in a trap might make, and I'd shudder and wonder what he was seeing in his night journeys into illusion. The other thing his cries reminded me of was my mother, who when I was a boy used to find herself attacked by malevolent spirits in her sleep, and the eerie moans she'd make in those paralysing nights were awfully similar in their character to the vagrant's yelping, in the sense that you could tell the sound coming from her half-open mouth was a shadow of the real cries taking place in some other plane of private experience.

Whatever it was the rag-man had going on in his alternate reality, the next morning, sitting out in the full sun with his eyes cast down into the tatters and stains between his knees, and with fresh vomit and drool drying in his beard, it was clear he had suffered deeply for having lived through his nocturnal picture show, and on those mornings I was determined to avoid his presence. The more ordinary madness began to get me down in that house on the street in St Peters, the darker my own thoughts became under the everyday strain of domestic discomfort, the more I started to take his dispiriting appearance outside our house as a portentous and unwelcome omen.

On nights when things were really bad at home in those married years, I'd go out into the park at the heart of St Peters and sit on the steps where there's a monument to residential misery built in memory of all the homes they had to buy out and bulldoze when the airplane traffic drove the whole neighbourhood crazy and reduced their property values to zero. I've never read into the facts of what happened to the residents there when the council bought the homes and replaced them with a park, but if you look closely at the sculpture of the giant couch they built in the middle of the park there, which I suppose represents a living room exposed to the planes that come flying so close overhead that you can feel the shake of their engines in your chest, and the vapour-slick belly of their fuselages looks like the smooth undercarriage of some airborne mammal, then you can see hundreds of crude little sculpted faces covering their ears on the couch like little Munchian screamers. I don't know much about sculptures, or any other art – not even obvious art like the kind an 1893 expressionist might paint. It's all double-dutch to me. But I can say that I've always liked the big couch in St Peters with its little screams, and I enjoyed being reminded by it of 'The Scream', which fascinated me even as a teenager with no interest in paintings or art at all. When I was young I read that Edvard had once written somewhere that when he passed over a river bridge at sunset on some long gone evening in Nice, he felt an infinite cry sweep through all of nature, and he sensed the cry would keep on passing through all of us for all of time like an eternal wave. 'There was blood and tongues of fire above the blue-black fjord and the city,' he supposedly wrote later in his diary about his walk across the bridge when he had the idea of his shrieking colours of blood and existential dread. If I were a painter, I would perhaps have wanted to paint blood-red tongues of fire above blue-black fjords, or some other local version of whatever a fjord looks like, but painting takes talent and practice and I have wisdom enough not to waste time with the latter in the former's absence.

In Renata Adler's book *Speedboat*, which many people who try to paint with words claim to love, she wonders about the people she sees on the streets who go picking out the scraps of things from bins and gutters. We've all seen these odd tinkers who bend down suddenly like machines and snatch at discarded butts with a heron's curled dexterity. Renata thinks these wandering recyclers might be writers trying to get through their strange confusions with the world and their own little screams the way writers do. I have never been one of those people on the street who are looking for butts and cans, and I find it a strange idea to compare the occupations of writing and scavenging, but then, I know that when Leonard Cohen's father died, Leonard claimed to recall going into the parental bedroom on the day of the funeral, opening the wardrobe where his father's suits were hung and inserting into the collar of one suit jacket a note he'd written. He claimed he could not recall what was written on the note, only the act of inserting it into the collar itself. It was all Leonard could do in the face of an awful internal commotion, the external cause of which he was helpless to affect. And he never really stopped putting those notes in the collar, so to speak. 'I followed the course', he wrote in one of his little notes, 'from chaos to art / desire the horse / depression the cart.'

I'm no longer a married man, no longer live in a converted bakery on a street in St Peters, but I still see the vagrant around sometimes, living rough on the streets of the inner west, though I don't live out that way anymore. Someone in Newtown told me his name one afternoon when we walked past him together, though I can't remember what it was. 'How do you know his name?' I asked, and she looked at me like the question itself was mad. 'I asked him,' she told me, shaking her head.

These days I'm only ever passing through those parts. Most of the time I'm out there to look after my son and to play in the park with him. One afternoon, coming home from a park in the inner west, not long after I left my wife and child, I made my late transition from ordinary, everyday madness into genuine lunacy at an intersection between Bonnyrigg and Badgery's Creek on Elizabeth Drive. The intersection where I first began to lose my mind completely was declared the worst in Sydney when I was a young man. Its notoriety was not due to the frequency of accidents occurring there, but a spate of carjackings that took place over a period of two months at the turn of the century. There were more carjackings at this intersection at that time than anywhere else in Australia. On a walk home from work at the plaza one afternoon, I saw the journos there, setting up their cameras to capture the scene. It didn't look anything special to me, just a regular set of traffic lights. I was coming home in my stepdad's tie and a four-dollar shirt and the clouds to the west were wild grey over the mountains. They put the intersection on the cover of the paper the next day, but it still didn't look like much to write about to me.

I think of this moment of newsworthiness whenever the subject of madness arises, even if I am the one who brings it up in the first place. I think it's strange that it was this ordinary but notorious place where I lost my plot completely and became a raving loon.

Like the stranger in Camus' novel, the sun was (sort of) in my eyes that afternoon when things warped inside. It was red and pink and setting over the distant Blue Mountains. I happened to be heading for the mountains because, having left my little family, I had retreated to live out there with a still-married couple of friends, who let me put my bed in their spare room because they were Christians who wanted to help people out when they could. I'd spent the whole day in Newtown, playing with my son on the swings and slides in Camperdown Park until we saw the trees were filled with stink bugs. My father always said stink bugs can send you blind with their spray so we left the park, though I don't know whether that is true about stink bugs blinding people, since no one else has ever mentioned such a thing to me, and my dad can exaggerate. There wasn't really anywhere for us to go after the park was ruined, so my son and I just sort of wandered around and looked at the graffiti and the people lying in the grass and on blankets drinking beers and smoking. Some dogs were going by and my son patted those and I said we'd go inspect the ice-cream shop but it was all shut up and he said his legs were tired. 'I'm half dead,' he said about his tired legs. What I really wanted was a beer, but kids don't go for that sort of thing and anyway I had to drive, so we just sat around for a while. When it was time to take him home, I got there just in time to be only a little late, but there was trouble in the doorway anyhow. It isn't easy to be calm and rational when you're dropping off your child and you're suffering from the normal sorts of disorders and you've got to be driving away as soon as the door shuts. It takes a lot of work to keep your composure, and I'm not really composed in the first place. I admit that I sometimes made it harder than it needed to be, and when his mother and I started to disagree about what a young man ought to experience to make him grow up strong and healthy of mind, she started to win because she'd been reading books about the subject, and so I just said, 'Well I don't need a book to tell me how to raise my son.' But I had to slam the door to get the last word in and I'm pretty sure that's not the right thing to do whether the books agree or not.

The sound of the door crashing into the frame, the empty windows on the houses of the street in St Peters, the slicked spiked hair of the cat sitting and staring from behind the weeds and bars of my old neighbour's yard. You know that high and mighty feline look they give you. 'What are you looking at?' I actually asked the cat that question. And the look of his smug yellow eyes and the smell of the paint factory on the corner there and my Dad's face when he was pointing out the stink bugs in his orange trees – these things kept playing round and round in my mind as I was driving away to the mountains. There was this bad pressure in the centre of my head. It was always there when the ex and I did any fighting, and nothing seemed to push it away except getting home and drinking in the spare room of my friends' house with the lights out.

I came to the intersection between Bonnyrigg and Badgery's Creek after an hour or so of peak-hour driving, and the pain was so bad I could feel it moving like a metal slug under the skin of my forehead. The lights had me stopped there for a minute. I looked into my rear-view mirror. There was a man in a green Camry behind me. I couldn't make out much about the guy because the sun was in my eyes, except he had dark shades on and his hair was slicked back. I was looking at that guy sitting there in his Camry, and I had an astonishing idea. It started slow and small, like a dot of dirt on the rear-view mirror that you've suddenly noticed, and since it blots out such a tiny portion of your vision you might not bother to clean it away for years. But I let the little idea sit there for a moment and suddenly it was all I could see. The idea was this: the man in the Camry with the shades and the slicked back hair was going to kill me.

I have never been a confident man, and I've had my share of irrational ideas. When crossing a one-way street I look both ways, when walking into the next room I have to check if my fly is still up and my shirt is still buttoned, when the barista asks my name I say 'um' before I come up with the answer. I've never been certain of anything more complicated than my phone number, and even then I can only recite it correctly when I say it with the usual rhythm. I can count the number of certainties I've ever experienced on one hand, and I've lost track of how many irrational things I've entertained. Once, when my younger brother was four, we were sitting in our kitchen drawing on scraps of paper with our pencils, and I heard my brother say 'bonsai'. When I looked over, I saw he was drawing a little tree on his piece paper. It occurred to me that no four-year-old boy ought to know what a bonsai is. Yet, I'd heard him say it with my own ears and could see him drawing a little tiny tree with my own eyes. I concluded that my brother must be a cyborg. For the next few months I kept close watch on him to see if there was any further evidence of his being a robot underneath all that chubby skin. But he never did anything else suspiciously clever like that, so I decided he wasn't a cyborg after all, or he was going to make a decent brother whether he was or wasn't and I might as well go along with the charade.

To give you a sense of how uncertain and irrational I can be, after I wrote the paragraph before this one I went to sleep, and woke when it was the middle of the night and saw the shape of a man holding a child in his arms at the foot of the bed. A rush of terror ran through the axons of my nerves but the terror sat side by side with an immutable incredulity of reason which assured my semi-conscious mind that the figure was only an illusion in the dark. Neither the impression caused by tired senses nor the reassurances of the rational mind were totally persuasive. Both senses and reason argued against my reaching over and turning on the lamp, which would have put paid to all argument about the matter. When I woke late this morning, both senses and reason maintained that the other had been under the influence of irrationality, with the superstitious side suggesting that it was madness to refuse what was evidently apparent, and the logical domain rested its case on the misleading nature of appearances.

But with the idea that the guy in the green Camry was going to kill me, I was for the first time in my life truly certain. I was more convinced of that idea than I am the order of the days of the week, the whereabouts of the sun when looking at a clear blue sky, or the surety that it is my own mind which controls the hands that are writing this sentence. In one long moment, the idea that the man in the green Camry intended to kill me became so insistent that my fingers began to tremble on the steering wheel and an odd moan broke out from my mouth.

One of the things I was surprised to discover about myself from this affair is that I really don't want to die. When I realised the man in the shades in the traffic behind was going to kill me, my foot came down hard on the accelerator and I saw myself as if in a film, flying and spinning around oncoming traffic at the intersection, dodging between the cars turning onto Elizabeth Drive and the startled faces of their drivers as they slammed on their brakes, too stunned even to consider pressing down on their horns or screaming out their windows.

By the time they thought of doing something like that,

I was halfway to Penrith, overtaking trucks and retirees and swerving in and out of the traffic lanes all the way to the turn-off onto Badgery's Creek Road. Hanging a left there I almost lost control and came to a stop in a wide spot of asphalt near an old fence with a long stream of flapping yellow tape tangled in strands of black barbed wire that had rusted into the branches of a eucalypt.

From there I sat and waited, scanning the roads in the distance behind me, watching the traffic passing the turn-off, waiting to see if the man in the shades would follow onto this quiet road, while I breathed in gasps and swallows.

From there, a slight rise in the general slope of the land, it seemed the whole of pastoral suburbia was spread out in a great green plain, and over the long stretch of fields and the farms on the horizon the clouds were glowing gold and lit with fire, an immense stillness and a deep silence, and power-station sentinels guarding the scattered sheep and dairy cows moving over the hills. In each of the three fenced-off yards by the main road the sky was mirrored by still silver ponds as deep and wide as pools. Maybe it was the adrenaline or the imbalance of chemicals racing through my brain, but looking upon those three bodies of water reminded me of a story I'd read many years ago of a scientist hiking through a hinterland wood and coming across a frozen waterfall with three columns of ice hanging from its cliff-edge. The scientist stood before the ice, dumbfounded, and as he fell to his knees his resistance left him, he had seen the face of God. I felt God's presence hovering high above the still waters of the ponds, in the immensity of the red and gold clouds, and trembled at this terrible force.

As a child I had dreamt one night of looking out the back windows of our house and seeing angels gathering in the night sky. They were hovering over the hills in great squadrons of cloud, and God, an enormous figure with a Zeus-like physique, rode at the centre of this winged caravan of clouds. He raised his arm, and sheaths of fire rained down from the angels' fingertips, and the homes and streets and the land beneath them exploded into eruptions of smoke and ash and ruin. In the clouds above the paddocks and plains while I waited for the man in the shades to come, while the scattered sheep limped between old tractors and dissembled cars, I saw God's presence, and there was nowhere to take cover from him, he was there watching how my small drama would unfold.

The light grew darker while I waited, trembling and sweating with my hands on the wheel, and soon enough I realised that the man in the shades was not coming. At first it seemed impossible to reconcile why he had given up his pursuit. I was certain that he wanted to kill me, it was not possible to be wrong about it. Like the movement of clouds, or the opening of a flower, my idea about the man in the shades began to change its dimensions into some new configuration. It was true – the man in the shades wanted to kill me, but he didn't necessarily want to kill me this afternoon, he would bide his time, torment my mornings, evenings, afternoons with a timing known only to himself.

Worse, he intended to torment me like God testing Job, he would take all there was of my life, piece by piece, until I'd paid in total for my sins. The terror this idea summoned in me was absolute. I called my ex-wife. 'Listen to me,' I said, 'someone is going to kill me, he's going to kill all of us!' I told her about the man in the shades, how I'd seen his intentions from the glimpse in my rear-view mirror. She listened, left a long silence after I'd spoken, and when she responded there was an odd calm in her voice. 'I think you need to call your doctor,' she said. 'Can you please, please promise me you'll call him?'

For a moment I pictured my doctor's office on the street in St Leonards, the leafy garden and the stone steps between the bushes leading into his practice, the settling sound of his voice as he opens the door and invites his patients in, the honest blue of his wide eyes. Then another thought overran this image of my doctor. It was the night my son was born. My wife was asleep in the double bed of our birth suite, the lights were out, and I was standing over the cot, watching the little baby breathe, his slight movements in the dark, and the smell of him in the room like sweet fresh dough. Earlier in the night, we'd heard screams and an alarm had sounded, bringing rushes of midwives and nurses, their raised voices and commands coming through the door. A child, only just born, had stopped breathing in a room up the hall, and the mother was wailing. They took both of them away, but I stayed awake, above the tiny bundle, watching the small movements beneath the swaddle we'd tried to make around him, putting my face close to the nub of his nose to be sure it was doing its job and bringing air into his little lungs.

'It's too late,' I decided to say to my ex-wife, 'too late for the doctor.' The idea that had coursed its way across my mind and announced that the man in the shades was going to kill me evolved its revelation one further time. With the same all-consuming certainty that had possessed me at the intersection, I realised that the only way to save my family was to kill myself. Whatever evil spirit animated the man in the shades made it inevitable he'd take everything from me, I knew it, but ending my life would just as surely put a stop to his devious intentions, and I'd save the lives of my loved ones in the process. 'Please,' my ex-wife repeated into my ear, but I said goodbye and resumed driving west. There was no need to hurry, my plan to kill myself was unimpeachable, and a great calm seemed to settle over the world. God, who was watching, would understand my actions, would forgive me for throwing my life away, he would see that it was out of love that I'd surrendered his gift of existence and he'd spare me from his wrath.

In Glenbrook I pulled into a parking space out front of the local hardware store, thinking that a Stanley knife would be an efficient tool for wrist-slitting. To make sure, I googled 'how to successfully slit your wrists'. A few websites in, I came across a statistic – only one in three hundred attempts to commit suicide by the slitting of wrists are successful. 'One in three hundred!' I said aloud at this discovery. 'But those are preposterous odds!' The thought of trying to cut myself to death and failing was intolerable – absolutely unacceptable and exactly what the man in the shades would want. An entirely different means of self-destruction was required, but I couldn't think straight in the car park of the hardware store, as two men in shorts and boots were leaning over a red wheelbarrow stacked with small tomato plants and their loud laughter was ringing in my head. So I gave up and went to my friends' place in Glenbrook, thinking I'd have a cup of tea and come up with a means of killing myself that had better odds at home.

Nobody was at my friends' place. Once inside, I locked all the doors and stood by the front window with the blinds pulled down, looking through the cracks at the empty street as the sun set and the jacaranda tree's long bare branches scraped the wall outside in the evening wind, sipping my tea and waiting for the man in the shades to come. For hours I stood by the window, sweating at the sight of every car going by. The house was so dark and quiet, I had no idea where my friends were, but I was glad they weren't around – it was not safe to be close to me. At some late hour I decided he wasn't coming that night, and crept quietly through the empty house and sank into my bed. It didn't take long to fall asleep, but when I woke it was still dark, and at the foot of my bed were three leathery demons, silently watching as I came to. I screamed and ran out into the lounge room, hitting the lights and shaking in the silent house. I'd no doubt at all that I'd seen them standing there, black figures with skin like the wings of bats, their tall bodies covered in monks' hoods adorned with bent crowns. I couldn't go back to my room and face them again, so I sat in a chair, with the lights on, and waited for the dawn, or the demons, or the man in shades to come.

When the dawn came I fell asleep, and stayed dozing in the chair until the front door opened and my friends came home. 'Hello!' Cate said as she stepped inside, her smile enormous, her arms held out wide in astonishment at discovering their housemate asleep in a chair by the front window. Tommy, her husband, lugged a bag into the house and smiled, angling his eyes to show them to me from behind his dark glasses. It is not my custom to assail people with bad news the moment they walk into a room, but I could not keep from speaking about my fate before they had even set down their bags. 'I have to tell you something,' I said, 'there is a man who is going to kill me, and my family, and it is possible he will come here and kill both of you too, if I stay, so to protect you all I am planning to kill myself, today.' They looked at one another. Tommy dropped his bags and Cate sat slowly into the couch. 'Who is trying to kill you?' they asked me in unison, and so I explained about the man in the shades in the green Camry, whose intentions were made clear to me at the intersection when I'd glimpsed him in the rear-view mirror. At first, they did not seem to understand the irresistible nature of this assertion, asking questions as if what they were hearing was unconvincing, but I expressed to them the depths of my certainty, and eventually they came to see how unshakably and immutably this circumstance stood.

Lunatics, I have found, especially when they are fresh, are often persuasive about the contents of their misconceptions. Thinking back on the discussion I had with my friends in their lounge room, I really cannot say what portions of the madness they believed – but I remember that when we had finished talking Tommy had covered his chin with both hands, and Cate's eyes were red and wet. Like a man sentenced to death, I said goodbye to them both and got in my car. Then I realised I'd forgotten to come up with a plan. 'Ah hell,' I figured. 'I'll just jump off a cliff.'

A long way from the highway, at a turn-off just before Leura, there is a lookout a friend once took me to. He was a climber, and knew the secrets of the mountains and its trails well. There are many places with strange names in that part of the world, The Blue Labyrinth, Paradise Pool, and Silver Cascades being some of my favourites. I don't know where in the mountains these places are, or what was the name of the lookout my friend took me to see, or why I thought of it as the place to go and jump off. On the way I called my mother and explained the situation to her, which seemed the right thing to do. She didn't think jumping off the cliff was a good idea, and instead she begged me to come and stay with her. 'I'll take care of you!' She insisted. I tried to explain that this would put her in mortal danger. She said, 'I've been divorced three times, you really think I'm afraid to die?' It seemed she would not be reasonable, so I had to say goodbye to her and hang up, and keep my mind on the mission at hand.

At the lookout things moved very slowly. There was no

one around, thank goodness. I figured if I did this cliff jump correctly, people might imagine that my final moments were bold and dignified, going into the undiscovered country like a stone tossed into still water, rather than what it started to become, which was a cowardly kind of hesitation, a sobbing and blubbering affair, where I stood beyond the fence over the deep blue-misted chasm of the valley with its immense green forests and whimpered and cried with shaking limbs. The idea, with all its perfect certainty, commanded me to jump, reminding me that this was the only way to save my family. For a long time I stood partially suspended over the empty air, the clear sky over the deep gulf between the lookout and the endless woods in the distance, urging myself to take the leap and get it over and done with. It is likely I was stalling for something like the following scenario to take place: my phone rings, and I discover my ex-wife's voice on the other end, and somehow, she talks me out of jumping because even though I know it is the only thing to do, there really is some part of me that does not want to die. Fortunately, that is what happened. 'Please,' she said. 'Can you just please ask your doctor's opinion on these plans of yours? If he agrees with you about this stuff then you can carry it all out.' 'That is a good idea,' I replied, stepped away from the edge of the cliff, and climbed back over the fence in a hurry as I thought again of his office in St Leonards, with its fern fronds and rose bushes out front, and the sight of his big, blue, all-seeing eyes and his waving hand beckoning me into his office.

For the next few days I slept fitfully, or not at all, and cowered under the covers in the spare room at my mum's place, thinking snipers were shooting at me from the street, and always seeing green cars, Camrys, Commodores, hatchbacks and station wagons circling the house as I watched from the windows, talking to myself about demons and the ghost in the shadows until my appointment with the doctor came. I touched the ferns and the rose bushes in his little garden, walked the stone steps between them and swung open the door into the dimly-lit comfort of his practice. I sat and waited by his door, and soon enough it opened, and he was standing there, waving me into his office, smiling and mouthing my name. In the calm quiet of his room he asked me how I was going. I told him about the man in the shades, about the demons and the snipers, about how the cars had been circling and the plans that were being made to torture me and test me like Job, and how God had appeared over the ponds at Badgery's Creek. I was explaining all this to Doctor Young, when something occurred to me about the whole situation, something I'd not even remotely considered up until that very moment. I stopped and said, 'Can I ask you something, Doctor? Does any of this sound, well, *crazy* to you?' He looked at me, adjusted his glasses and said, 'Yes, it does.' I sank back into the softness of the chair and felt as though I'd broken from a trance, as though I'd been an actor playing a scene for days and the director had finally called cut. 'Oh, thank God!' I said to him, almost laughing, 'I'm just crazy!'

To encounter madness is as ordinary and natural an event in modern life as it is to discover dew on the morning grass. Manic tempers, obsessive vexation, insomnia, psychomotor retardations and bouts of bed-ridden anhedonia are everyday maledictions. It is easy enough to get used to these interruptions in other people, and, if you're lucky, you can get used to them in yourself. I'm writing this odd account on the night of a blue winter moon. My neighbour is playing 'Three Bags Full' on his pipe, and late-night semis are grinding their compression brakes between the many speed humps in the street, while my brother, invisible despite the orange light of the city to the east, assembles his telescope out on the grass. I had tried to warn him while he was sliding the lenses out of the Styrofoam slots, 'You will wait a long, long time for anything much to happen in heaven beyond the floats of cloud and the Northern Lights that run like tingling nerves.' But he told me blankly that the heavens were teeming with happenings that poets don't have the patience to comprehend. It's rare to have clarity out here in the suburban winter, so close to the city, and he's struggling to see the fat Jupiter moons suspended in their rows between the stars. He has to catch them now, they are already drifting outside the scope of his enormous contraption – and his eyes are going, and the surgery to save them is more than anyone I know can afford. Besides, there's a resignation in his heart that permanence is not part of God's plan and decay ought to be respected. Upstairs my mother is trying to sleep, but the new medication keeps her awake, the flow of blood in her arteries rings in her ears. I've started smoking again, which gives me something to do on the stairs outside at night in the cold. There was an ad when I was a young man where the surgeon general would splice open a smoker's brain and aim a dribbling clot at the camera. It makes my head-spins seem ominous when I think of this. Upstairs the History Channel is blaring, an Englishman is talking about Freud and the interpretation of dreams to a woman who isn't in the frame. They are in the doctor's death house, where my ex-wife once took me. The death house is full of totems and ornaments. There's a prosthetic jaw in a cabinet by the door. The tour guide stopped by this antique device and told us that the cancers which grew in the doctor's mouth were sent by the unconscious to keep itself from being discussed abroad.

When Dr Young asks me why I've reverted to smoking, I'll say that the nicotine makes a nice oscillation in the dulled Paroxetine calm. His owl-wide eyes will be on me, as he leans over his notes, and he'll know I've rehearsed this answer, as always, in some pre-emptive attempt to seem worthy of salvation.

I can't see my brother any longer, he's a vague movement in the dark. Far to the south of the city, my father is sleeping in his little room, attached to a monitor strapped round his chest which reads his pulse in the night. We are all attached to our little lives, and it is right to keep clinging on. But, like any addict, the former lunatic must keep abreast of uncommon rhythms, tics and changes in pressures around the head and in the chest. I go in when the smoking is done and look across the threshold of my room. I hit the switch but its wires have become crossed, no light comes on and the room remains dark. To no one, I say aloud the strange lines of a Pink Floyd song that always make me happy, replacing only one word for my own amusement: 'There's no dark side of the room, not really, as a matter of fact, it's all dark.' This is not much of a joke, but it's a sign of life, and, as ever, that is enough for now.

FATHER AND SON

After my son was born his mother and I spent nights watching over his cot, patting his back while he cried and wriggled and dozed and woke again. The floorboards outside his room were creaky, and we learned to step with such a slowness of motion as we left his room that it sometimes seemed as if we weren't moving at all. Were the boards to creak despite our sly stepping, his eyes would shoot open, a piercing wail would sound, and we'd rush back into the room and pat and rub the strange crying creature we'd created until he surrendered again to sleep.

Just outside his bedroom, where the boards were most sensitive, was an IKEA bookshelf where a collection of classics with decaying covers my wife had inherited from her paternal grandmother was kept. On one occasion, as I was leaving his room at a glacial pace, I grabbed a title from the array of decrepit spines and opened the book up to discover it was Gogol's *Taras Bulba*. I hesitated outside the doorway long enough to read the opening scene where the old Cossack, Bulba, greets his two sons with insults and jeers upon their return from the Academy in Kiev. The older son responds by threatening to punch his father in the head, and a donnybrook between them erupts. The mother – fat, kind and ugly – shrieks from the doorway, 'Look, good people! The old man has gone mad – he's pummelling them!' Bulba tells his wife to shut her gob while the men are bonding, and after a few blows to the ribs and head, father and son embrace each other, and a feast is ordered amidst a flurry of kisses. Despite Gogol's claim following this scene that men like old Bulba 'could only exist in that fierce fifteenth century', it did not take much of an imaginative leap to see the mad Cossack as a close analogy for my own old man. While I was not yet a Bulba myself, the thought that one day, the fitful, chubby creature in the cot behind me might want to rain proverbial blows upon my head in some suburban driveway was terrible to contemplate – the thought of wanting to strike him back even worse. Just at that moment, my weight shifted, and the boards beneath me creaked. My son's mind-bending cry erupted from the darkness of his room, and all thoughts except rushing to his aid and patting him back to sleep were obliterated.

In those early months and years, my wife and I were coated with dried drool and milk stains, the bins were overloaded with nappies, and a purchase from IKEA was interminably being assembled somewhere in the house for the growing child's amusement. Too tired to read, let alone write, we watched television, slumped into each other on the couch like a beanbag of body parts, straining to hear the muttered dialogue over the constant radio static of the baby monitor. What little social life we had was soon reduced to trying to listen to visitors speak while a toddler crawled over our faces. It got worse, of course, when his mother and I split up, and for the next few years I'd get up early, fold up the futon of whatever spare room I happened to be living in at the time, drive out to my wife's house through the drudge of peak-hour traffic, and take over my son's care while she went off to work at the university.

I was always up for games, and tried to be a playful father, but after three laps of chasing my son around the kitchen table, my heart and lungs began to give out, while his stubby legs kept pumping from out the holes in his nappy, until he would overtake me, and I'd collapse into a chair, telling him between gasps of exhaustion to go on without me. I have never liked sunshine much, but on grey enough days we'd go out to the park and kick the ball. It always ended up in a tree or down a drain, and my boy would look at me with disappointment as I reminded him that I had an antipathy to heights and an aversion to enclosed spaces. Some days we attempted field trips, but more often than not we'd come to the foyer of some museum or the aquarium in the city to discover that I didn't have the dough to get us in, and we'd circle back while I explained that whatever we'd come to see would have likely been underwhelming anyway. I deployed cultural criticism to save money – circuses and zoos mistreated animals, museums had colonial associations, Hollywood movies were propaganda for American exceptionalism, electronic devices were peddled by manipulative technocrats, and sugary foods were toxins perpetuated by corrupt corporations – but he learned to see these rhetorical positions as self-serving pretences for depriving him of liberty. Most days I'd spend a few hours half asleep on the couch, watching television, while he stumbled about in a dance of boundless energy.

Above the television in the house in St Peters at that time was a 3D print his mother had hung on the feature wall, where our boy's face was shaped by the clumped clay readings of some newfangled scanning machine that had painted his portrait while he was still in the womb. He would come running over just as I was about to nod off, leap up onto my lap and squeal in his whistle-high voice, 'Daddy Pirate! There's a booger in my nose!' Sometimes I was so tired that instead of bothering to find a tissue I'd squash his clear nostril closed, put my lips up to the squishy stub of his nose and suck out the oily cluster. The tangy blob would sink slowly down my throat and congeal to a stop in the centre of my chest, and I'd have to hit myself like a broken vending machine to keep it moving. He'd wince and slap my cheeks trying to get free from my grip, and his skin was soft as silken sponge-cake, and he smelled like soapy sweat. Occasionally he'd grab my head with his soft hands, covering my ears, and stare into my eyes like he was peering directly into my soul. My wife explained that this intense interaction was called 'facial tracking', and it was part of every infant's development, but I knew he was some kind of earthbound angel, and each time he looked at me like that a dizzying wave of pure love would pass though me like a blast of God's own radiation.

Once he was beyond the age where every utterance was a novelty, he began to take pleasure in singing rhymes with altered lyrics, like 'Old McDonald had a bum! E-I-E-I bum!', for hours on end while he stomped about the floorboards of the house, his blonde hair like a slick mop of straw that had been dropped onto his cantaloupe head. 'You've got your mother's hands,' I used to say to him, and he'd give me a flash of his lightning-bolt-blue eyes and punch me in the crotch, running off into the kitchen just fast enough to dodge a retaliatory kick up the backside. The days were listless beyond bearing, and I knew I should have been writing. For as long as I could remember that had been my reason for being, and there was plenty of time to do it while also being a body in the room as my son was growing. It would have taken no extra effort to take notes for some new work of fiction, read the classics, or study a foreign language – but most afternoons when I walked out the door of the house I did so without having had a single sentence pass through my mind, and this realisation would lead me to make a quick stop at the pub on the way home, enough to get a rush of alcohol through the bloodstream, and I always left with a couple of six packs in my arms to get drunk on, and pass out with an open bottle by the bedside. Most mornings I woke up hung over, and would need to spend time reclining to shake the grim lethargy of intoxication out of my body, telling my son 'Daddy's feeling sick again' while he ran around banging fire trucks into Duplo towers.

One morning, during one of these recovery sessions, I changed channels to find the Prime Minister on the television, standing before a Christmas tree and making some kind of announcement. The sound was down and his teeth looked like clippings of steel cemented into his mouth. Across the room, my son had climbed up on the kitchen bench and was peeking under the closed blinds to watch the grey morning rain slop onto the roof of a car yard across the Princes Highway. I took out my phone to relax and take a read on Facebook, and discovered everyone was tagging '#illridewithyou' in the wake of a siege in a Sydney café. A distant cousin with three children had posted 'As a mother, I have to ask, what in the FUCK has this world come to!' and hundreds of people had given her the thumbs up.

On the television, a few seconds of footage of the gunman was now going around and around on a loop. He was scuttling sideways like a crab with a human shield and a black backpack for a shell. A scarf inscribed with a language-other-than-English was wrapped around his head. If the television had been unmuted, the newscaster would have told me that the script said 'We sacrifice ourselves for God', and I would have struggled to understand the meaning of the message, or why someone might pick up a gun in the first place and take themselves out to a bright, gold-trimmed café in the city where the chocolate is served in a fountain, put black banners in the windows, and wait for a SWAT team to come and kick in the door as smoke bombs filled the room with stinging grey clouds.

'I love you daddy, *on Triple J!*' my boy said, still facing the grey rain outside. My wife's cats were behind the television, sitting below the framed 3D scan, watching dust and dirt fall from a hole in the ceiling, where, somehow, a sparrow had made its nest. I knew there was no way the cats could get to the bird, but the shrill sound of its chick, and the cold interest on their feline faces as they looked up at the call of this little creature was sparking inside my skull like the blooming seed of an aneurism. I got off the couch, went over and helped my son stack up some towers, and he handed me a fire truck so we could crash into things together.

When my wife came home I went for a walk on Newtown's King Street and imagined the many cafés all under siege by invisible gunmen, inflamed with mad grievances, ready to swallow up the active-wear parents and their innocent babes in their sports utility strollers. I stopped at the end of the footpath near the Bank Hotel to let a young blonde girl on a scooter go by, and for the first time, without knowing precisely where the tangible essence of it might lie, I saw something I'd always suspected other people recognised instinctively, just by dint of being human. I could see for the first time why all these people were scrambling about the streets with their coffees and phones in their hands, or lumbering into bars to get loose and sloppy, and I could see why signs and banners were painted in bright colours on the store fronts, why the young people had dyed their hair and rolled up their sleeves to show dark tattoos, why the roads were packed with passengers on buses, and workers in hi-vis uniforms were digging down under the pavement or tightening powerlines, why the bums were begging for coins with their dogs' heads on their laps, why the window washers were carrying dribbling squeegees near the traffic lights, and why the cranes moving over the skyline like steel behemoths were swinging their loads through the fading light of the grey afternoon. It occurred to me that this endless rumbling of energy and motion was done for the sake of tiny, growing children, all to keep their miniscule hearts beating and expanding, and their little lungs moving sweet warm exhalations of breath out between their thickening bones. Corrupt and debased as the world was, pernicious and petty and evil as its carnivorous ways were, this vast human activity and its enormous complexity was running up against an unimaginable and inexhaustible threat of extinction, so as to keep small crying babies growing and suckling their mothers and gulping at bottles in the ordinary shade of houses and units and cafés and parks all over the city, from one generation to the next and on and on into eternity.

The girl on the scooter rode down King Street and out of sight, and it occurred to me that I'd spent so long clinging to the consolations of a life lived in fiction that I'd allowed myself to miss the point of life completely. Through all the ordinary misfortunes of existence, I'd used the idea that one day I'd be a writer as a kind of transcendental promise – if report cards snitched on my laziness and caused my parents to adopt a disappointed look, or if bullies assailed me on the bus and threw my school bag in some hard-to-reach place, I'd go through the motions of an injured ego, but there was always the icy secret hidden deep inside that one day I'd escape from the crude confines of the real and into the open expanses of fiction. From the very beginning, I had trained myself to renew my flagging spirits with the thought that someday I'd set down on pages a work of redeeming colour and shape, and I'd come to see the lives of people around me as a kind of abstract resource to be used to perpetuate the arrangement of my words.

To see for a moment the city's reason for being – the unbroken chain of causality from which it had all sprung and continued to grow – cast all fear of gunmen and loonies out of my mind. I saw in the evidently indefatigable spirit of ordinary life that there was no reason ever to be worried about any particular detail of the world, which was another way of saying that I would never need to write again – no need at all, since no particle of this strange constellation of the real world would ever need to be revised or redeemed, not by me or anyone else. Men who moved like crabs, holding guns to people in cafés, had been around as long as cats had licked their lips at baby birds; agitators, maniacs, subversives, nihilists, vandals, barbarians, creeps and con artists were always at the gates, and yet, the collective will was overwhelmingly on the side of mothers and fathers and babies needing to be nurtured. For all their faults, love and care had always won, or the world would have ended, and none of what was around us would hold any meaning at all. Despite the implacable horrors and stupidities of earthly existence, all would be well so long as mums and dads stuck to the plan. Having had this idiot's epiphany, I walked into the nearest bottle-o, bought a couple of six packs and went back to the spare room of my cousin's flat, unfolded my futon and drank both packs with a crooked smile of amazement on my face. All I had to do for the rest of my life was be a dad.

To say that this feeling of release from the impulse to write about the world endured would be a lie, but it lasted, in oscillating degrees, at least until the day after a recently celebrated royal wedding. The wedding became a family affair for us. 'I remember when Diana got married to Charles,' Mum said as we sat around the coffee table in the lounge room with the fire blazing in the combustion heater against a mild chill. 'Your father and I got dressed up and we drank champagne and watched it on the telly.' It felt good to be part of a family tradition. We'd assembled in our small home in the western suburbs, and on the coffee table Mum had placed Saos, cheese cubes, pickled onions, sweet gherkins, chips and corn-dips for my brother, his fiancée, myself and my little son – now all of seven – who sat with his head bowed towards his device, having declared the wedding stupid and dumb, while we drank wine from flutes and waited for the Queen to arrive in the church with the princesses and dukes in their gowns and hats.

With much shame I report to drinking so much bubbly in my enthusiasm for this royal family function that I could not remember a thing about it in the morning, and had to scoop my son up in my arms with a pounding in my head that made it hard to walk in a straight line out the door, and up the driveway towards my car in the bright golden augury of the clear May air. My son didn't seem to notice, intent still on his device, and I buckled him into his booster seat and proceeded east, towards his mother's house on the other side of the city.

As we drove into the tunnel that dives below King Georges Road, we came to a standstill in the gloom punctuated by brake lights. Even with the windows up, as we inched forward with the blockade of cars and trucks, a harsh chorus of sounds began crashing around us, a loud thrumming racket, as though an enormous swarm of locusts were cascading through the darkness. I switched on the radio, remembering that it was sometimes customary for the tunnel operators to commandeer car stereos to broadcast messages to drivers when there were any incidents that might impinge the free flow of traffic. There was nothing there but the buzzing distortion of static. My son remained oblivious, his eyes mesmerised, and I could see the luminosity of the screen reflected in them, his pudgy finger prodding at the objects on a virtual plane. 'What's going on?!' I said aloud to no one, and craned my neck to look further over the halted procession of shuddering vehicles under the low and dribbling impassivity of the tunnel. It was simply impossible to be sure what was causing the hideous noise that was pulsing through the closed windows of the car. It seemed to me, delusional as it sounds now, that for all I knew, at any moment a roaring avalanche of pests might besiege the halted traffic we were in, and swallow us in our cars, devouring our flesh and leaving metal and bone in their wake.

My skin was dry from the wine I had drunk, my eyes were puffed and red, my organs felt swollen and my hair was thin in the lime-coloured light that bounced off the mirror from the dim lamps on the greased walls of the tunnel. A headache pulsed through my whole body from my temple to my toes, and I had a sense that the terrible wave of insects would crash through the windshield of our car any moment and consume us with its million tiny mouths. I resolved that should the plague descend upon us, the only thing I could do in the seconds remaining would be to turn to my son as he sat in the back seat and assure him that all would be well on the other side of life, to give him some consolation to withstand the inevitable horror of being eaten alive by the forces of nature.

What could a man in a car, sitting in the gloom of a tunnel underneath Sydney with his young son in the back seat playing a game on his device, possibly have to say to prepare the boy's spirit for the experience of being eaten alive? Perhaps he would wish to communicate, with some gestures and a tone of voice he has reserved for a time of great urgency, the significance of an experience some years now in the past: a memory of the boy's arrival on this earth. The precise memory the man in the car might wish to translate to his young son would begin on the morning after he was born, when, being told by other men that it is customary to celebrate the birth of a child by smoking a cigar, the man had left the confines of the hospital for the first time in many days, on his own, and had gone to a nearby beach to fulfil this custom. The man had found a cheap cigar in a service station, bought a lighter too, and stood on the steps of the boardwalk near the beach. There, looking out at the breaking rhythm of the surf, he attempted to light the cigar and smoke it for several minutes, uncertain how to successfully perform either action.

The sky was clear and the sun was warm and the beach was crowded with people in their late-November undress, and at last – the rich, muddy taste of the cigar becoming wet and tart in his mouth – the man managed to generate a cloud of smoke he felt was fitting enough for the ritual to be satisfied. He experienced a mild dizziness, and was about to discard the still-burning cigar by squashing it against the bricks of the boardwalk, when he noticed the crowds of people on the beach beginning to point at something moving in the waves. Two whales, a mother and her calf, bobbed on the surface, the high white sun licking their slick black bodies as everyone stood transfixed on the sands. The man stumbled forward, seeming to be the only person moving on the scene, astonished at what he saw – the slow, careful nudge of the mother whale as she breached from out of the depths, her immutable bulk caressing the slick body of her calf, their gentle forms seeming to glow in the diamond gleam of the water spraying into the air around them.

The man, who had not slept a moment in the forty-eight hours before this vision on the beach, saw in that mammalian tenderness some echo, obviously, of his own circumstances. When his child had been born the night before, he had watched the soft naked creature emerge from the swollen, bloodied body of his wife with an open-mouthed amazement. First, after hours of struggle and strain from his wife and the midwives, the child's head had come forth, a strange alien shape, then the small fat body was moving of its own accord, bobbing on its mother's breast in search of the dark circles of her areola, the mother asking in disbelief through his cries and motions, 'He's alive? He's alive?' as if it were unthinkable to her that a living thing had appeared from her body, the flesh of her flesh granting new life.

Soon the doctor handed the wet, wriggling form of the boy into the man's arms, and although the nurses had told him he would cry when his child was born, he had not believed them. In the hospital room, with the baby jiggling in his shaking arms, he felt for a moment as though all his ancestors were standing to applaud. It was not a sensation of pride he felt blowing through the tight confines of the hospital room, but a great release of joy – another life, with all its potential tragedy and comedy, had come into the world, and the man himself had played his part.

When, of course, no wave of locusts arrived, and the traffic began to clear, my young son and I proceeded from the tunnel into a pale blue Sydney morning. When we had driven far enough away, I pulled over to the side of the road to catch my breath. My son didn't notice, his attention fixed to the game on his device, in which he was building castles, block by block, occasionally speaking to inform me how much improved his structure was becoming in the world he was moving through, especially in relation to the peasants around him who were building rudimentary block houses of their own.

When I'd relaxed enough by the side of the road we proceeded through the quiet calm of the inner west, neither of us speaking until we came to the driveway of my wife's new house. 'Time to go,' I said. Without looking up, my son told me he wasn't finished. I told him there'd be plenty of time for building things some other day, took the device out of his hands, and reached into the back to unbuckle him from the booster seat. 'Let's go,' I said in the tone of an order, but he grabbed hold of my arm and said 'I don't want to go; I want to stay with you.' We looked at each other for what seemed like a long time. It was impossible for me to think of anything to say to him except, 'You can't.' He let go of me and squirmed out of the car, running up the street beside his mother's house and standing with his arms by his side under the shade of a conifer tree. There was golden light now, the sun caught behind a cloud above the street, and a young man was walking his dog on the opposite side of the road. I was hoping this stranger's presence would help to tame my son, thinking he'd be embarrassed to be in a stand-off when someone else was there to see it, but he stayed still under the tree, with an expression on his face that I'd never seen before. 'You gotta go to school in the morning,' I said, not sure how that observation related to our current situation but hoping it would have some effect. He shook his head and said, 'I'm not coming.' Neither of us spoke. I tried instead to wave him over, adding 'I'll see you tomorrow' when the waving proved futile. When the young man with the dog rounded the corner and disappeared from sight, I ran up the hill, reached out, and snatching my son up, carried him to his mother's door. He was heavy, and he hung onto me while I walked up the stairs and handed him over to her. She hugged him close and shut the door, and I went down and sat in the car. For a while I sat there and listened to the empty street. The device I'd snatched from his hands was on the passenger seat, and I picked it up to inspect the building project he had been so keen to complete. He'd created a long tunnel, and navigating through it I came to a small cottage where there were two beds. One had a sign next to it with my son's name and the other had a sign beside it reading, 'Dad'. There was a chest next to our beds, and he'd put food and supplies of axes, swords and shovels in there. On a wall he'd hung a painting of a flower in a vase, and the other walls were lined with bookshelves. Out the window there was a blocky garden with a picket fence, and some chickens laying eggs, and beyond that was a lake surrounded by trees and the sun going down behind a mountain top.

The drive back west was easy, there was no stopping in the tunnel. Back at home, my brother and his fiancé had left, and Mum was sleeping on her recliner, the television still showing highlights from the wedding. I got a text from my wife to thank me for trimming my son's nails, and I sat on the couch with a beer and drifted into a state close to sleep. A vague awareness that my mind couldn't quite grasp overcame me, and a dream unfolded through a heavy, all-consuming fog. When I woke, I couldn't remember the dream, only that it started with my son and me being back in the car. We were parked by the side of the road near the end of the tunnel and the only sound was the dim rumble of cars going by, and the clicking of the blocks my son was assembling upon the castle towers on his device. His neck was bent towards the screen, his brow creased in concentration, a worried look in his eyes. Through the window behind him there was an enormous construction being built, the beginning of a new highway which would solve all the congestion and change the nature of the city. There had been protests, people were upset about the tunnels being dug under their homes, the noise and smell of the machines and the earth being dumped in great mounds by schools and playgrounds. My son's steady finger dropped a careful block onto his virtual tower and when the startling intensity of this movement was complete, I changed the gears with one hand, turned the wheel with the other, and accelerated into the stream of traffic heading east.

THE WHISTLEBLOWER'S LAMENT

At this midpoint on my life's journey, the only advice I have to offer the reader is that if you should awake to find all sanity expunged, you should have prepared some means of being taken to a quiet street off the Pacific Highway in the suburb of St Leonards. There's a clinic there with a cool garden of palms and ferns out the front, and when you get there, ask to speak to Dr Peter Young. I understand this sounds like absurd advice because, although this plan of action has worked on several occasions to restore my own fevered mind to proper working condition, it is ludicrous to propose every person coming across this odd account will be free to engage the talents of a sole mental-health professional who, despite his prodigiousness, is but one man. But the fact that there exists even one head-shrink who possesses the capacity to heal a mind as humbled beneath all reason as my own, ought to serve as a message of hope to anyone who finds themselves lost in the bleak hinterlands of internal disorder.

For those distressed enough to go looking for help when their inner workings start misfiring, but unfamiliar with the lay of the mental-health scene, it should be pointed out that the first port of call is your local general practitioner, who cannot personally help you with your madness, but will know someone who can. Some readers of this essay might be lucky enough to have an established relationship with their GP, a doctor to whom you and the family have turned in times of misadventure, disease, and the occasional illness. Then there are those who have no idea whom to consider at all when they get ill, let alone whom to speak to when they become sick in the head, and have to resort to googling some variation of 'local doctors' in order to initiate first contact.

Many years back, when I first became desperate enough to go looking for help, the results of just such googling was a certain medical centre, an establishment sitting at the heart of the popular inner-city Sydney suburb, just across from where a tapas bar now abuts an anarchist's den, and every Saturday the markets sell dreamcatchers, and a mystifying line of Japanese tourists assemble for watermelon cakes at the little bakery on the corner, and the cops roll over the square by the medical centre doors with their lights silently flashing so couples will part, coffees in their hands, to let the squad cars roll on into the uptown traffic. Incidentally, at the time I first found it online, this medical centre happened to be one of the worst-rated general practices in New South Wales.

Not wanting to malign their reputation unjustly, I stopped for a bit after writing the previous paragraph to check whether things have changed at the medical centre since those days. I offer the reader these accounts posted online by patients who've allegedly attended the place within the last year:

(1) *'The experience here was more painful than the condition I went to get checked out...it was like speaking to a bus driver about rocket science'*; (2) *'The receptionists here are extremely rude and seem to have a deep hatred for all that is good and holy'*; (3) *'After she finished taking my blood pressure she mumbled, "you're fine now get out". As I got up to leave I made a comment about the appalling service I received. The good doctor simply looked at me and screamed "close the door you stupid boy!"'*

To say these reviews are representative of the general consensus is an understatement, and on the afternoon I first discovered this much-maligned centre, worse reviews than these were the predominant impression online. There was one important caveat to these negative reports – one still observed in the current litany of online reviews – a strict agreement across every account that there was a doctor who served as the centre's one redeeming reason for being. It happened Dr Lee was the GP I encountered when I first went looking for help, or perhaps this account would have an even bleaker ending than the one I'm intending to tell.

The receptionists at the inner-city medical centre are treated ungallantly by online reviewers, but through the haze of sickness I admit to having found their stoic detachment an ideal model for just how the rest of the world ought to be. They exuded a perfect indifference as they processed my Medicare card, a solemn and impassive air – just the kind of unobtrusive human interaction a confounded mind tolerates best. I clung to the edge of their reception desk like an error-plagued automaton reporting for rewiring until one of the women, a short blonde with ice-blue eyes and snowy cheeks, handed me a slip of paper with my name printed on one side and a doctor's on the other. She told me in her thick Slavic accent to take the slip up the double flight of creaking stairs and slide it under the closed door of the doctor in Room 4. I did as ordered, taking the groaning stairs two by two and slotting myself between the other hunched patients arranged in opposing rows of grey chairs against the wall. Next to me was an old white-haired man whose withered hand clutched the head of a cane, and across from us were two broad-shouldered women with matching mermaid tattoos and little piercings set in their cheeks.

The slip of printed paper I stuck under the door marked 4 was eventually sucked up by an unseen hand. At this weird sight the old man nudged my knee with his cane and with a cavernous smile said, 'It's a bit like a brothel this place.' Under any other circumstance I might have been tempted to feign a false air of offence and say loudly enough for the rest of the patients to hear, 'What do you mean a brothel? Why would I know what a brothel is like?' simply to amuse myself at the old man's expense, but, as people like to say these days, I was *unwell*, so there was nothing to do but nod and stare and the old man gave up on me as a means of distraction, and turned his attention back to the spot in the wall between the two women.

The magazines in waiting rooms rate somewhere close to a leper's undies on my scale of things I don't want to touch, but if you look at their covers for more than a second, stacked on the table, you don't need to pick them up to stay informed – Prince Harry was back in his Nazi outfit, the Kardashian sisters walked the beach in string bikinis looking candid and Junoesque against the blue California waves, and couples of whom I only vaguely knew, Ashton Kutcher and Mila Kunis perhaps, were said to be breaking up in Tinseltown. There was framed art on the waiting-room walls, but not knowing much about the subject I couldn't pick the style or say for sure that they had one – a forest scene, purples and pinks in the skyline, horses, they might be, on the hills. Notes in all caps stuck on the doors warned us to turn off our phones for the sake of sensitive equipment, and a young mother with thick brown boots thumped and thudded her pram backwards up the long double-stairs, the baby asleep inside despite the bumpy ascent. When they both reached the top the mother's plump face was slick and red and she collapsed into an empty chair with a definitive grunt.

The various doors opened every so often and a name was called, and the chairs would rearrange and new people came stomping up the stairs to take their place in the collective waiting. The situation we were in was a little like the funeral-parlour scene in Camus's *The Stranger*, or so it struck me for a moment, though thinking on this bolt of connection I could not explain to myself where exactly the analogue resided. A plasma screen hung on the wall above door number 3, on which was playing a repeat of a morning show called *Today*. The hosts of this program and their roaming reporters were investigating the creation of the world's largest lamington, which had been brought into being in a parkland in the suburb of, Olympic Park. Through one of their intrepid reporters the excited hosts interviewed the chef, a dark-haired, nervous-looking woman, who seemed unsure how to explain or to feel about her strange masterpiece.

A door opened on the far side of the hall and my name was called. I sat in the busy little room with Dr Lee and saw precisely why she alone was spared the scorn of the online reviewers. When you place your distress in the hands of others, you can take on the hysterical bearing of some small mammalian critter caught in a snare, a prey creature whose heart is likely to burst if external intervention is not tender enough. Dr Lee seemed to know by some amalgam of instinct and experience just how to treat me in my derangement, and an aura of clinical motherliness emanated from her every pore, so that I could confirm the intensity of my illness to her by beginning, in an unseemly fashion, to cry. It didn't matter that I'd lost all continence in front of this stranger with a stethoscope, who was handing me tissues at regular intervals. She consoled me with the knowledge that she had in her possession a form developed precisely for those who report to their GPs with my symptoms. On this form there was printed a chart asking the patient to indicate their state of mind on a scale where (1) is best and (10) is worst. The questions on this form include: How would you rate your interest or pleasure in doing things? Or your capacity to concentrate on tasks, such as reading the newspaper or watching television? How positive do you feel about being with friends and family? For once in my life I was able to assess myself a perfect (10) across every dimension of measurement. The doctor, radiating something like an impassionate love, continued to pass tissues as I regained some composure while dealing with the quiz, and when that was done she read over the answers and said, 'Have you made plans to kill yourself?' She met my eyes and added, with an empathic look, 'I have to ask you this.'

Yes, I told her, I had been thinking perversely of a film I'd seen at the house in St Peters – *Encounters at the End of the World* – by the director Werner Herzog. The scene that had preoccupied my thoughts was the one where Arctic explorers simulate snow-blindness by putting buckets on their heads, and attempt to navigate by way of a rope wrapped around their waists. The buckets they are wearing to obscure their vision have crude faces painted on their sides, and as the disoriented explorers bumble about in the falling snow – getting nowhere and tangling into each other, tying themselves in knots with the rope that is meant to keep them together – the old Bavarian director intones these words in his monotonous, existential manner: 'At first the participants seem to be heading in the right direction. But soon the man in front veers off course, pulling everyone else with him. This one mistake soon leads to another, and in moments the entire group has wandered hopelessly off course. The primitive faces on the buckets lend their futile attempts to navigate in the simulated darkness a dimension of sinister comedy.'

It's humiliating, trying to explain a fetish for dying you have growing inside you, but it came out of my mouth as unresistingly as the tears had done, and Dr Lee, who cupped her chin in her hands and took on the appearance of someone keen and sincere, listened while I explained the scene where I intended to be found, under the prayer flags strung across the courtyard of the house, on the sun chair beside the succulents, a bucket on my head with a face painted on it and my pale wrists slashed wide open, bleeding a deep, wine red – a little river on which to sail into oblivion. I told her I had thought of nothing but this mock tableau for days and nights with growing certainty, and the wild colours and motions of that courtyard scene were more solid and real to me than the walls of the doctor's office, with their bright charts of the human anatomy with veins dissected, and advertisements for vaccine injections on posters besides shelves with curved metallic contraptions whose utility I couldn't begin to imagine.

I've heard it said that the first thing a lunatic loses is their sense of humour, and some psychs will tell you the best indicator that a patient is returning to sanity is a growing capacity to laugh at jokes of their own devising. When I first watched the Herzog film with the experiment in snow-blindness in the darkened house with my wife and child upstairs sleeping, there was something hilarious about those Arctic explorers' blinkered bumbling, but there was nothing funny about it when I sat with the doctor. She seemed to be watching my face carefully and I became self-conscious that there might be an ugly tell in its expression that she was interested in understanding, but when the time came for her diagnosis she explained that she was not the doctor I needed, of course, since I was unwell in a particular sense, not merely ordinarily broken or damaged. She provided the contact details for another, subtler practitioner, and so began the weird saga of my time in the mental-health game.

Destitution afforded me one advantage – when Dr Lee sent me off with the names and numbers of people and places to help fix my head, I took with me a government voucher for a dozen free consultations. The first address she'd given me was for a clinic that charged next to nothing in a nearby suburb where pregnant women, newborns and lunatics all mingled in a wide waiting room under a series of staircases and lifts. Glass walls showed untended gardens between the offices and halls, and busy nurses and clinicians passed through the swinging doors with a maddening frequency. On my first visit there an older man in a flannel shirt and dirty sneakers sat beside me on the waiting-room couch and in a drawling voice said, 'I know you, don't I? From Port Hedland? That job out at the mines there. Haven't seen you in a long time. Must be twenty years, yeah?' He carried on with knowing winks and smiles, and each time I came to the clinic he'd be there, ready to resume our reminiscence.

I nodded along while he found ways of keeping our conversations flowing without relying on any corroborating remarks. It was convincing, after a while – who am I to say I didn't work in the mines – and in his voice was a gentle, rumbling enjoyment which made it difficult to dissent from the assertions he made about our former life together in the towns of the north-west.

The counsellors there shipped me along to a Redfern psychologist whom I took to be some kind of Freudian. On occasions she would suspect me of making one of those notorious slips of speech that are supposed to reveal something hidden about your unconscious, and her eyes would widen in astonishment. 'Do you realise what you just said?' she would ask me, and it seemed to me that she was satisfied we'd made some kind of progress. One afternoon I walked into the waiting room and took my seat while a man with a tool belt prepared to glue the name of the clinic to the wall across from the reception. The man made his way through the first word of the clinic's title without much trouble, putting glue on the back of each letter and then making a careful estimation of how far along on the sky-blue wall it ought to be stuck. It was when he got to the word 'psychological' that his nerves began to show. He looked around for some point of reference, but the walls were blank. When he stuck the Y after the P, I made my move. Pretending to get up for a magazine from the table by the wall, I instead stooped beside the man in the belt to warn him in a whisper that he'd made an error in the order of letters. He said, 'Shit', then pulled the Y from the wall, taking a small eggshell collection of paint along with it, and for the rest of the day I felt euphoric for having done some good for my fellow man.

With her long auburn curls and her crossed fulsome thighs, the Redfern woman and her Freudian leanings made me think of the notion I'd gotten from the ubiquity of psychiatry in American movies and television, that falling in love with your analyst was an essential part of the therapeutic process. If there was anything happening at all in my sessions it wasn't love, and if it was, there was no fidelity. She saw other patients, I saw other doctors. One of those was a woman who worked in the city, across from the State Library on Macquarie Street, whose office was located on the third floor, and sometimes we'd endure the indignity of riding up in the lift together in total silence. She was a serious psychiatrist, and seeing her wasn't cheap. None of it was free anymore; I'd used up the vouchers in a matter of months and the help I was now getting from the series of doctors was eating up the small lump of savings I had.

One afternoon, waiting for my appointment and admiring the library across from the psychiatrist's building, I saw a big man in a suit sitting under a café umbrella whose voice was loud and whose companions were also big men in suits who joined him in speaking at a conspicuous volume. There was something familiar about the man in the suit; his face was large and his chin was thick and his slitted eyes looked weary in the glare. I might never have figured out who he was if a car hadn't stopped in the middle of the street, from which two men, also in suits, leaned out and began shouting, 'Hey Twiggy! How are you mate?' The slit-eyed man in the suit gave a short wave and smiled politely and the car drove on with the horns of the cars delayed behind them giving the interaction a carnivalesque effect. It was strange, seeing a man worth billions of dollars sitting at the café outside my psychiatrist's building. It seemed to me that a man like that and whatever I was ought to reside in two different dimensions. 'I'm going to mention this to the doc,' I said under my breath, but sitting upstairs with a plastic cup of water and the serious doctor sitting across from me, I forgot to bring it up. That session she diagnosed me with Borderline Personality Disorder. 'Most people who have your condition end up dead or in prison,' she told me. 'You're doing well when you look at it that way.'

For a while I collected books on the subject of BPD, as we sufferers call it. For anyone considering reading up on the subject I'll save you some time and provide you with this summary: *you're the worst prick there is and there's nothing you can do about it.* Reading up on BPD can give you the impression that the utility of this category of mental illness is the ability to assign it to people who present with the various characteristics of insufferable arseholes. If you feel empty, have a terror of abandonment, leave a trail of disastrous relationships in your wake, turn on the ones you love, are enslaved by your impulses to a self-destructive degree and lash out at the world with capricious behaviours, then you're a prime candidate for the BPD party. There's no cure, no medications, just endless cognitive therapy and a dishearteningly low chance of living anything resembling a remotely functional life. One slight silver lining for me was that I'd only borrowed the books from the library, and so was able to forget the dispiriting information they contained once they were returned.

At the Black Dog Institute they told me the problem was bipolar disorder. The receptionist there smiled in a way that encouraged me to think there was nothing wrong with me for turning up, which was more attention than most clinical practices can boast, and she brought me into a room with dim lights, where a touchscreen computer was set into the wall like an exhibit at a museum. The computer knew my name, and it asked a series of questions much like those I'd seen on the form with Dr Lee. When the quiz was over, the screen flashed a big emoticon smile and told me to wait back in the foyer. The receptionist gave me an encouraging look when I told her I'd completed the test, and she informed me that an interview had been set up with one of their doctors. The good news, she said beaming, was that the doctor I was scheduled to see was a very important person, one of the top people working at the Institute – a professor, the director, or both. The wait wasn't long, and I was ushered into a room upstairs to meet the important doctor, a tall man with a loose suit and a checked tie that hung down into his lap.

He introduced himself and asked me to sit, then turned his attention to a file one of the other psychs I was seeing had sent him. 'Paranoid tendencies', the important doctor scoffed.

'Whatever that means!' I wasn't sure if he was talking to me or simply making a professional observation, and I didn't want to be rude and watch him read, so I sat still and stared out the large window to my left, watching the cars passing on the busy roads outside, and the tall gums trembling in a sudden breeze, while he kept his chin thrust down into his neck and read over the report. He soon put this document aside with what seemed like disdain and read through another item on his desk, one I assumed the computer in the wall downstairs had produced. He read this without comment, making a few mysterious grunts and placing the back of his pen in his mouth till he was ready to begin conversing.

He asked some questions after a while, crossed his arms and said in an officious voice, 'Well, based on the information we have here, it looks to me like your diagnostics indicate something between Bipolar (1) and Bipolar (2).' He explained that if we were to think of Bipolar (1) as being the category to which the extreme cases of the condition belonged – those who suffered delusional manias in which they believed themselves to be Christ reincarnated, for instance – and then considered Bipolar (2) to be that category of sufferers whose manias find them binging on eBay and engaging in Twitter feuds that cost them their jobs, then we'd have to consider the symptoms presented in the reports he'd just read to be somewhere in the middle. 'So that leaves you more of a Bipolar (1.5),' he said, and as he did so two pigeons collided with the large window to my left in an explosion of feathers and twisted wings. 'Jesus Christ!' The doctor laughed. 'Suicidal birds!'

All these institutes and counsellors and Freudians were excellent people, but I didn't give many of them a chance, in part because I'd been raised to regard those who worked in mental-health care as charlatans and kooks in need of the remedies they purported to peddle, and I considered those who sought the assistance of these frauds and fools to be losers and wackos with too much time on their hands and not enough common sense. I'd gone from that crude cynicism about the field to spending almost a year with shrinks of one variety or another on a weekly basis. Though the sessions often involved some sort of breakdown, breakthrough or revelatory release, the curative wonders didn't quite seem to stick, and I'd wake up each morning, as always, back in the same wild miasma of confusion.

This therapeutic dialectic might have gone on with an irregular perpetuity if my wife had not intervened. She didn't say it directly, but there was in her look the expression of a woman who had grown tired of cohabiting with the hobbled creature that called itself her husband, and she must have been sick of watching me lurch around the house in a kind of accelerating discombobulation. Also I was an unemployed mooch. She called on her friends and asked them to recommend a decent place to send me to. Many of her friends were veterans of the therapy scene and I was directed by one of them to the quiet, leafy street off the highway in St Leonards whose reputation was spoken off with the same empathic reverence you'd lend to a hip wine bar or a private swingers club.

It was a long drive, across the bridge, and a nuisance trying to find parking under the fat trees that loomed over the footpaths in the metered streets of St Leonards, but as I walked through the shade of the garden at the front of the clinic, a queer shiver of ease enveloped me like a cool, calm breeze, and in the low light of the waiting room, beside a water cooler and a stack of old *Who* magazines, I sat beneath a Whiteley-esque painting of a beach, with a curving coastline and frothy slashes of white where the sailboats and surfers broke the dark water's surface.

I was the only patient there, and assumed the standard waiting-room trance until a door swung open at the end of a hall from which a tall thin man in a pinstripe suit stepped out and halted for a moment, expectant and prepared, like a porter coming through the gated entrance of a railway station. He looked at me from across the hall, gave a small waving gesture and said my name in a voice no louder than a whisper. We shook hands in the doorway, and he bid me to take a seat in a fat plush chair across from his own squeaking seat. The blinds were low, but I could see a shaded garden out the window, and behind the doctor were neat shelves of volumes on subjects with titles appropriate for a man of his position. He smoothed his lap and placed in it a clipboard loaded with sheets of lined paper. His brown hair was cropped short but it had a prickly look, like the frayed bristles on an old toothbrush. Most dramatic of all were the taut lines of the doctor's face, the long trenches at the front of his cheeks, which might have had a severe effect were it not for his enormous eyes, set behind round glasses that his long-fingered hands would occasionally touch as we exchanged the usual things that pass between a nutcase and a doctor on a first date.

In what way our conversations differed from any other therapeutic session I'd experienced is not easy for a layman to pin down, but just as my encounter with Dr Lee had taken on a maternal dimension from the first instance, so my interactions with Dr Young contained a subtle trace of father and son. Like it had been with my dad when I was a boy, I paid Dr Young a visit once a fortnight, and he'd listen to all that had happened since we'd seen each other with an evident interest. My father always had the perspective necessary to interpret the immediacy of my childish impressions, and the words to affix them to some grand narrative of the bigger world. Dr Young supplied this same wisdom for me, and in his sessions it was possible to learn, not merely to talk – to confess and be consoled.

'The consensus,' he explained during one of our chats, 'is that to categorise a person as "having" borderline, or any other personality disorder, is a less useful way of thinking about diagnostics.' Apparently the data collated by the top clinicians indicated that it was more useful, and truer, to think of people as exhibiting behaviours that can be correlated with a spectrum of personality disorder traits. In short, the best minds in the field had concluded that we are not our disorders, and they don't constitute us. This was encouraging news, and on some level it seemed like common sense.

Whether it was part of Dr Young's role as an encouraging father-figure or not, he appeared to beam with pride when I went back to work, or wrote some piddling essay, or even expressed an idea in an unusual way. I asked the doctor to help me return to the PhD I'd left years before. When I quit, they'd warned me there was no coming back, but I hoped a letter from Dr Young stating I'd done so under internal duress rather than mere foolishness would have some kind of incantatory power over the university administration. He said he was happy to help, but wanted to know a bit more about the subject.

In polite company, it is common knowledge that asking a PhD student to explain their research is a regrettable *faux pas*. In all but the most exceptional cases – none of them coming from the humanities – the student will instantly deflate with insecurity, not sure they can speak to their subject without reviewing their notes, or crippled by the suspicion that no one in the world could possibly be interested in the abstruse subject they'd foolishly married themselves to. Against this overwhelming reflex to self-sabotage, I managed to mention two literary critics, Bob Hodge and Vijay Mishra, who had written a book in the 1990s in which they describe Australian literary culture as an attempt to deal with the guilt and illegitimacy of a settler-colonial legacy by constructing a mythical Australian authenticity. All I wanted to contribute to their diagnosis was to argue for augmenting their concept of guilt with an idea of shame – since shame, unlike guilt, is not bound up in a need for forgiveness: it cannot be expunged. Shame, as the affect theorists have it, teaches us what we value, whether we know it or not, and displays it for the world to see in the capillaries of our cheeks and in the bowed posture of our heads. If we deny shame's bitter bite, or attempt to evade its withering touch, we risk pathologising ourselves and those around us.

There was nothing extraordinary or revolutionary in my description of the project, but something about this idea of shame piqued the doctor's attention. At any rate he said, 'interesting ideas,' as though he meant it, and I didn't disagree since none of them were mine anyway. We got back into the swing of our therapeutic relationship, but there seemed to me some lingering preoccupation with shame in the air, and the doctor pressed his pen to his chin while we talked.

Not long after this conversation all our appointments were shifted from Tuesdays to Wednesdays, and when I asked why during our next session I was shocked by his response. 'I'm no longer doing my other job,' he said. I had the sense he wanted to leave the subject alone but the idea of my doctor having a second job was too much of a curiosity to be left unexplained. It turned out Dr Young happened to be the shrink overseeing the mental health of every asylum seeker detained by Australia, on- and off-shore, and he was leaving the job to blow the whistle on the toxicity of the entire detention system. My preoccupation at the time, rather than the moral and ethical dimensions of what the doctor had just said, was merely to marvel at the thought of Dr Young flying out to those island camps with barbed-wire fences and armed guards, seeing patients with their mouths sewn shut, or those who were refusing food in protest.

It occurs to me that I can offer a second piece of advice for the reader: when Dr Young returns your sanity to you, don't assume your troubles are over. With his guidance I got my mind back and along with it came work, family, friends and other benefits. I didn't mean to stop going out to the leafy-gardened clinic in St Leonards, and I never intended to stop seeing Dr Young, but things were so well that it just sort of happened. In our last session before I gave up on therapy, we chatted as usual, and he was happy to hear the university had let me back in on the strength of his letter. 'All's looking well then,' he said. 'That's really great news.' There seemed to me something just under the surface of his taut expression, and he was holding a long finger up to his lips as though some secret was close to being spoken. We shook hands at the end of the hour, and just at the last moment, with both of us standing in the doorway where we'd first met, he said: 'I have something that might be of interest to you. The journalists at the *Guardian* – they're good people. When you go home, keep an eye out for an interview I did with David Marr. You'll find it interesting I think.'

Mad people, even those like the old Holden Caulfield who lie in their hospital beds monologuing about their brief time in the arms of lunacy, are never free to forget about madness, lest some fresh fever lay its insidious claim on their minds. I learned this the ugly way, forgetting all about what it was to be mad, forgetting all about the doctor and his cryptic remark about some interview he'd had with Patrick White's biographer. The receptionist called and left messages about making new appointments, but only the desperate have time for therapy and I wasn't in despair anymore. At some point, when the distemper and antipathy roared back into me with a vengeance, I left my wife and child and moved in with friends and began hiding away from the world, and was by then too embarrassed to let the doctor know how badly things had fallen apart. The more this shameful fall was hidden the deeper the pit became, and it wasn't long until this downward trajectory erupted into a full-blown bout of psychosis. Had I not returned to Dr Young's care, and faced the pitiless disgrace of my circumstances, it would have been the death of me.

Somewhere along this spiralling collapse I came across an article in the newspaper about the doctor. Months after he'd spoken to the papers and been interviewed by David Marr, when he labelled the government complicit in the use of torture against detainees, and after a *Lateline* interview where he defended the credibility of workers who were sacked and defamed for speaking out about the abuse of children they had witnessed, the news broke that the Federal Police had tapped his phones, stolen his metadata and questioned colleagues who dared to speak to him. Little wonder that those in power would target Dr Young, he had the temerity to say that the Australian government had deliberately permitted the harming of vulnerable people in order to dissuade them from considering Australia a viable destination. I watched his interviews on YouTube soon after reading about his violated privacy. It was strange to see his deep-set blue eyes and his taut expression at full size and in colour on the pages of the paper, stranger still to watch him sitting across from David Marr, both tall thin men in suits, and hear my doctor saying, 'The detention system is designed to make people suffer.' I recognised the room; he was in my chair. The bookshelf behind him was the same one I'd sat beside during our many conversations, and I could imagine the cool garden through the window that the camera couldn't see.

Towards the end of the interview Dr Young tells David Marr, 'When you go to Manus Island, and you walk down what is called "the walk of shame", between the compounds, and you see the men there at the fences, it's an awful experience.' Marr replies by asking, 'Did you feel shame?' and the doctor tells him, with his large eyes unflinching, 'Absolutely, yes. And you have to feel shame. You have to experience that – you have to understand that – to understand what that feeling's about.' Marr, with his hand rubbing at his temple asks, 'Is that why you're talking now?' And the doctor says, 'Yes.'

The doctor put me on Paroxetine for life, and Seroquel carried me through the psychosis, and now every morning after breakfast I crack open one of those pill boxes old people get so they don't lose track of their drugs. No doubt the doctor has recovered from the violation of his privacy, though he seems more reticent than ever to talk about his whistleblowing phase. What good his actions did is not for me to say, and I wonder if he doesn't despair at how little anyone outside the *Guardian* seems to care. If it gets him down, he doesn't say, and I suppose it's none of my business, since I'm only there in his leafy little clinic for my own sanity, and for anyone who needs help with that kind of thing there's no one better in the mental-health business. If I were the sort of person who leaves reviews online, he'd have all five of my stars, and I'd leave a line or two saying, 'If you're out of your mind, this is the guy to go see.'

A PORTRAIT OF THE ARTIST IN RESIDENCE

Fond memories first: the grey-skinned trees and the hill-dimpled fields of the Kingswood campus crowded up to the windows of empty classrooms, the idyll outside bisected by the distant murmur of the Great Western Highway. Our group would meet once a fortnight in those eerily quiet and disorderly rooms between the bustle of tutorials where Marshall McLuhan quotations had dried onto the whiteboards and I admit to rolling my eyes at the others when they buried their heads in notebooks or read deeply from their manuscripts. We were typical undergrads I suppose: a girl named Allison who was ostentatiously in love with the 'bohemian' boy, Eddy; two tiny twins from the Mountains who synchronised their outfits and plaited their hair like characters from a children's cartoon; a shaggy bearded laddie from Kingswood who wore hipster glasses (this was in a time long before the term hipster came to mean almost anything to do with the white middle-class world);

and a revolving host of wannabe poets and posers who so closely resembled one another that they have become unified in my memory.

To be sincere with you, I thought I knew more about every available world than all these comrades combined, on account of being beaten, repeatedly, by skater-skinhead-homeboys and meth-mangled housos on the streets of Liverpool in my youth, and also because I'd trawled through the mania of Henry Miller's classics in the university's Werrington library between semesters, alone on the empty hills of the campus while the others spent their free time playing pool at the uni bar, drunk, discussing sustainable ethics between the cracking clop of the balls and their timid hollering at the bar staff about the patriarchy. All they knew about literature, I reckoned, was how to make cutting remarks on Hemingway's machismo.

One night, I was coaxed into the social world by one of the pixie-sized twins, who said, slinging her arm up towards my shoulder, 'Stop being so negative, it's such a clichéd attempt at seriousness through cynicism and it's just sad – y'know there's a lot going on that you can't even imagine, can you? You won't learn anything stuck in your room like a hamster in a colon.' In the bar, name forgotten, Eddy scoffed when I mentioned loving *The Old Man and the Sea* for its flagellant misery. I didn't mind him scoffing at my readings, but the next thing I knew his tobacco breath slid into my nostrils; he leant towards me on his pool cue, like a gargoyle clinging to a doorframe, and he said, 'Hemingway's problem was that he was afraid he'd never be as much of a man as

Gertrude Stein.' *What did I care about Hemingway?* I wondered, looking at the grin Eddy bore me as he moved back towards the pool table; Papa was just another headless horseman as far as I was concerned, but to say something like that about the man – something Eddy had no doubt stolen from a YouTube debate between Martin Amis and Terry Eagleton – shook me around like an eight-ball.

The light in the room was almost as loud as the hip-hop classics on the playlist (all black music was played ironically in Penrith back in those days). Next to a dance floor the size of a coffin, the twins were sitting on stools and they nodded in solemn agreement about Ayn Rand having nothing to offer re the problems of the blooming twenty-first century – a subject Eddy had meandered into. The shaggy-faced hipster could confirm this perspective, having recently read an article online about Late Era Capitalism and Slavoj Žižek's theory of divine violence which said pretty much the same thing.

It was possible I was just jealous, lacked charisma, but then again, I wasn't the only one who left early that night: Dani, the person I've held back from describing so far, as if it were some sort of secret, in fact was a true book nerd, whose cold command of the English canon made her the de facto head of our group. Earlier in the night, she took a dart from the board on the wall and told Eddy, whom she was taller than by a head, on account of his terrible posture and her thick Blundstone boots, 'The cult of the self is a shallow grave, and Rand was pushing on an open door, far as that goes – but I doubt anyone here has read a single word, outside of a title, or inside a cover, of one of her books – specially not you, Ed.' They all laughed with her, softly, supposing it was a joke, except Eddy, who rolled up his sleeves as he skulked to the bar and pawed at it, timidly, like a tiger who'd leapt and failed.

Dani and I left together – coincidentally – that night; she took her leave by the back and I went out the front, unnoticed, our paths intersecting in the dark, which had somehow consumed the sound of our footsteps. She started when we first saw one another in the shadows and said, 'Jesus, you scared me,' her eyes narrowed with suspicion.

'He scares me, too,' I told her, not sure if it was a joke, and instantly ashamed of having said it.

The moon was in every window of the empty buildings on the campus, and the strange squat lanterns along the paths were filled with the silhouettes of dying insects. In an unspoken agreement – negotiated with careful oscillations in our pace – we walked to the end of the road together.

'I hate that twit,' I said to her, referring – I hoped it was clear – to Eddy. She didn't say a word, and now the sound of us walking and the armada of gum trees beyond the edge of the campus felt oppressive. I took a long look at Dani's pale profile in the dark but the night had arranged her curled blonde hair so as to obscure every clue from me, and I tell you that didn't seem fair, and the walk went on in silence until at last I said, 'I have to go to the train station.'

For a moment, I thought she was about to laugh,

though I wasn't quite sure why she might find a comment like that amusing.

'Good luck,' she said without looking, and turned, without so much as a farewell wave, down a path through the park on her way to the dorms and I let out a sigh, suddenly aware of a painful feeling, as though my shoulders were carrying an enormous weight.

The next week we met as normal. There was a game we played as a collective in those chair-scattered rooms with the bald light flickering above us and the air-conditioner blowing like the burner of a hot air balloon from the ribbed vent in the corner. It was Dani's Game – a house-rules adaptation of Exquisite Corpse in which you were asked to 'write a sentence, fold the paper, pass it on' until Dani decided it was time to read. I didn't think it was much of an exercise. Dani – being a woman stepped directly from a Jane Austen fan club – didn't think much of my sentences, so I thought. She crossed her legs with a careful pull at an ankle-length skirt and her toffee-thick curls shook and her bosom was strapped tight to her chest beneath a lime-green top. In the case of Dani, it feels right to use the word 'bosom', since there seemed to me something out of step with time and language about her, either too late or too early in existence for my thoughts and words to brush against without dislocating, becoming archaic. She unfurled the group's resulting narrative and read it aloud – it was always her job to read things aloud – and the outcome, as always, was an elegant nonsense of prose all the way to the last syllable. I detested how repetitive each exercise became, how gentle and domestic – and how co-operative everyone tried to be – because I was dumb and young enough to believe there was something worthwhile about Miller's descriptions of winged lead erections and obsessed with the fields outside filled with ghosts on the run from history – which was the sum total of Australian literature in my cynical readings of Henry Lawson and Christos Tsiolkas.

Indeed, in the mode of cynic, I made much sport of Dani with my girlfriend at the time, a Greek Anglo girl with long black hair and eyes dark and evil enough to make me want to hold on to her in the night – the kind of girl I liked in those delirious days.

Outside in the car park after our group meetings my girlfriend would have her Commodore running for me, the 'done-up' exhaust shuddering like a pawing lion on the crest of the hilly campus, and as we'd ricochet onto the highway she would say, 'Tell me, Pendragon, what happened in your stupid group this time.' I'd tell her whatever absurdity Dani had ended on, for instance, according to her, that Nabokov had told his students that the most essential requirement for becoming a great reader was a sense of their own spinal column. My girlfriend, whom I don't wish to name and who, for some reason, gave to me the titles of British kings, would expose her crooked teeth as she grinned at these accounts, smiling to herself while I watched the university receding in the passenger's wing mirror, my thoughts straying for a moment to Dani's dangling blonde curls and her pale blue sternness, like a shallow pond on a spring afternoon. My hand wound its way into my girlfriend's hair and onto the pale skin at the nape of her neck, while the uni was swallowed by the accelerating distance.

But I did not tell my girlfriend about the time Dani came to my sentence when the afternoon light was low, and, by God, in front of the whole group, hesitated. It was the final meeting of that feeble cohort, and the exchange between Dani and me was something not to be shared. It all went as clockwork, up until when she unfurled the corpse as always, standing at the front of the class with the rest of us arranged in chairs like her personal scholars, hand-picked for the honour of following every elegant moment of her precise pronunciation. But this time, how I tripped her up good! In a moment of electrified rebellion I had invented, though it is hard to explain it now, a sentence I was sure would be a spanner in her proverbial works. And I was right! For the briefest of moments I had her frozen as the ice-man in his tomb! It is embarrassing to me now, but I tell you, Dani's sudden halt in narration seemed at the time a tremendous victory for an undergrad like me, who was ashamed of coming from nowhere and having read nothing. It's hard to explain, but I'd never met someone like Dani – who seemed unlikely to strike anything unexpected in her life, and who would sail forever across the surface of existence, seeing the universe divided, however arbitrarily, into the ocean and the sky as she passed over it with an even keel…Anyway, that's how I thought it was with Dani; and when she halted, I felt like a great fish who had learned to crawl, just for a moment, from her sea into her sky. The class was quiet and the slightest wriggle of panic made itself known on every blank face in the room. Eddy alone was willing to break the quiet – he crossed his arms over an Elmo-buttoned hoodie and furrowed his brow and said, 'What's wrong, Dani?' Dani mouthed the syllables I'd written and I knew she was struck by something sickly, something devilish. I might as well tell you the truth, although it doesn't make for good reading. I'd written: 'Satan punched the horse in the head.' The twins laughed when she said it aloud, and then Dani read it again to herself. The group – I don't know how to explain this – suddenly appeared to me a mass of lonely bodies (except perhaps for the twins) in which each saw for a moment that they were deceiving themselves if they had ever thought, even for a moment, that the world they could see and hear and taste was there to be shared with anyone else. Perhaps I was overdoing it, but I believed it was a good lesson for a room full of writers. In any case, the contagion of shame flared through the room like fire, and the way the sun was setting made it seem as though the classroom was beginning to blush.

Dani's brown eyebrows, which were slowly sinking, started to twitch, and the others shifted in their seats. She thought it over. The twins looked at one another, and the bearded boy in his hipster spectacles glanced over their thin rims at me with a quizzical affectation, unsure which way the wind would blow.

'What does it mean?' Dani asked, her hand still clutching the accordion manuscript our collective had created.

'I don't know,' I replied.

She looked around and her eyes were filled with a heaviness that might have been annoyance.

Dani cancelled the group. She shut it down for all time. The others filed out. Eddy with his arm around Allison, the twins and the hipster with their heads low shuffled off towards the uni bar to work out where the world had gone wrong. By another unspoken agreement, Dani and I stayed until it was just the two of us left: she sat on a desk, arms folded over the Exquisite Corpse, crushing and cradling it all at once as I slowly rose from my seat.

'Why'd you end the group like that?' I asked her. 'Can't you put up with one ugly sentence?' I tried to keep eye contact, but her eyes were too blue and the room seemed to get heavy with the light leaving the sky and weighing on us alone, so that our reflections appeared on the windows like parallel witnesses to our exchange.

'Look at where and who you are,' she said as I picked up my bag of *Sexus*, *Plexus* and *Nexus*, nervous she might recognise their shape and see through the whole affair. 'You're not a new thing, you're a fossil of the old world – you and every man-child like you, and, for your own sake, change – before we all get bored to death.'

Dani and I never saw one another again as undergrads. Except in my dreams – where, for no reason, for nothing to do with what had happened in the anaemic past of that memory, Dani's pale phantom would walk the streets of

Liverpool, past the slowly rising apartment blocks and the burning council chambers and the cemetery gates, and up the small mountain toward my house with its high view of the surrounding suburbs. I'd roll in the damp sheets and toss my head, and she'd follow me into Westfield parking lots and Chinese restaurant alleyways (sometimes in nothing but a green raincoat), her curls tinged silver in the moonlight and the light of her eyes like the curved edge of a spoon held up to the stars. She would stand in judgement at the head of my bed some nights, and pace the halls of libraries in ruby-coloured shoes. I thought, in waking life, of contacting Dani. Her name occasionally appeared in the Australasian Literary Society mailing lists, or on academic conference tables. In the café strips of Newtown's King Street where the sun was always setting and spilt-red twilight cascaded upon the rooftops, I thought once or twice I'd caught sight of her curls, disguised by a new style or updated to suit the season. It made no sense, and I could not change with the times.

All this would have come to no more than a wishful pornography but for an email that came my way a few months ago. The email was nondescript, full of formalities. It asked me, on behalf of the University of Wollongong, to come and be an artist in residence for their writing program. This was not surprising. After all, my collection, *A Dozen Doorbells on the House of Time*, had won the Premier's Award for New Writing. Since that win the invitations had come thick and fast and I, overwhelmed, stayed in my room and deleted them so as to convince myself that they had never occurred. The nondescript email from Wollongong University would have been no different, but the name at the bottom gave me occasion to halt the cursor above the little digital garbage can. It was signed, sincerely, by Dani – now, apparently, a senior lecturer in English. I closed the trap of my laptop and shivered so hard that the knots in my spine cracked. I rose from my bedridden slump with a thrill of dread and ecstasy.

'We can offer accommodation, at the campus lodge, should you require it.' A strange sentence that stood out as somehow enigmatic amidst the propriety of the rest of the email. Or was I reading wrongly, confused by my own suppressions and dreams? Even now, I am not sure if there is something meaningful about that sentence, but nevertheless, it thrilled me to find it in my inbox. Immediately, my mind filled with fantasies of seeing Dani again – this time, both of us adults, accomplished, seasoned and wise.

As it turned out, I was the only man, woman or child at the lodge during my stay on the oddly isolated island of Wollongong University. A security guard in dark blue uniform towered over me at the entrance to the campus and made me repeat my name three times before going upstairs into the huge concrete expanse of the administrative office to find the keys for my accommodation. When she returned she sternly handed me a card and pointed to a number underlined on it. 'That's the number to call if you need any help,' she said, almost threateningly. She was vague, too, on directions, and I circled the campus three or four times trying to turn down the right road towards the lodge.

The keys fed me into room number 6. The keyring included a large metallic disc, perhaps to prevent it being treated carelessly, engraved with a dog's head that also resembled a dove. On entering the apartment I threw down my bags and stripped off all my clothes, and ran naked and flapping up to the bathroom mirror as if to catch it by surprise; but what would you know! It surprised me! With the weak light of the late afternoon behind me, I was alarmed by the glow of my own muscularity, thought it for a moment a stranger, and in a panic, hurled a flurry of punches at the reflected figure who, after the initial shock subsided, became, in my mind's eye, a critic named Stephen Triste who had treated me badly. I hated him and his stupid sentiments. Often we would fight in my head. Always I won. In Triste's Twitter picture he looks solid of jaw and thoughtful – hand curled around his chin to demonstrate the weight of his mind at work. I wasn't sure how the fighting would go when this image was the extent of my acquaintance with him. Later, at some sad affair at the Writers' Centre in Rozelle, I saw that his profile picture was one of those magic moments in his life when he had looked good. In motion, as he descended a long staircase in that old colonial relic, his jaw was a wispy thing and his shaved head balanced like the bulb of an unburnt match propped atop a fleshless framework of pencil-thin elbows, knees and neck. After that vision of him – plodding down the old staircase with two complimentary cupcakes in his hand and a lanyard around his neck, like a puppet in a noose – he fought poorly in my fantasies, his wild swings bouncing off my head, and I would go so far as to say that the fantasies weren't fun any more. Triste wrote in his review of *A Dozen Doorbells* that I risked rehearsing the basest of masculine clichés. What a thing to write! Only a man as thin and frail as he was could write such drivel!

When night came upon the lodge, I lay on the made bed, having written my lecture for Dani's students, and I rolled into a dream of chasing Triste through the science quad at my old high school, with the September sun blinking at me through the crow-crowded ghost gums. In the dream I was long-haired again, a young man, soft with baby fat, and I grinned as we ran through the breezeway past the toilet blocks, and Triste, a miniature version of himself, had Sophocles or something stoic tucked tightly to his chest. He was beginning to wheeze with asthma and terror, and he hoped, I knew, that the mysterious dignity of ancient times would bleed from the book into his cowardly heart, or at least transport some dimension of his essence into the long gone past, which, since it is only written down in books, seems so much less shameful than the living nightmare of a boys school in Liverpool with spikes and barbed wire wrung around its head like a crown of steely thorns. There was no intent in my heart to catch him, only to herd him out onto the sports field until we both collapsed into the buffalo grass with the pure blue above us – me laughing tears of happiness, him crying into the grubby earth and beating his bird-boned fists into its hardness. That's all, to lay there for a while, history rewritten.

When I awoke from that dream, I didn't know whether it was still the first night at the lodge, or the second day. The curtains were drawn and the clock was unplugged. My phone was dead and I couldn't find the charger. The lecture notes lay on the table beside the bed. They were, I realised with dawning terror, an indulgent litany of jokes in bad taste. I promised myself I wouldn't swear during the lecture on this occasion, since it always shamed both myself and the students, and of course Dani, too, would frown on it, but I knew somehow that I would do it anyway.

What a strange thing! I dressed and gathered my notes and went down the stairs with my feet echoing off the stucco. It made me turn back a few times to see that no one was following behind, and I felt, stupidly, great pity for the maid who must go up to my room on those stairs soon, only to see that the lone guest did not wish to be disturbed.

On my way out I hesitated at the double doors of the lodge's conference room. It was on the ground floor, right by the entrance, and it was locked, but my room key worked it open. It would shame me greatly to tell you why I opened the doors, but I might as well be honest – I secretly hoped to see Dani waiting for me inside. She was not, of course. Inside there was a long table with little speakers in its centre; ten chairs, all out of fashion by several decades but well maintained or underused, some scratches along their wooden surfaces the only sign of life; and an old stereo behind glass in the corner. The lake outside the room, which I'd spent some time staring into on first arrival, was still too dark to make out, but its watery presence seemed to press up against the lodgings in the darkness as if it might make a move into the dreams of guests – dreams in which the whole squat brick building would perhaps slump sideways towards the lake and sink cartoon-like beneath the mud.

I sat at the head of the table, finding by the wall something to plug my phone into, and felt like a chieftain's body at a conference of ghosts before I noticed a tattered dart board displayed on the hip-high cupboards. I plucked out one of the darts and sat back down at the head of the table to toss it across the wide empty room – the green fins whirled and the dart's needle sunk uncannily into the bullseye. What a shot! It truly was one in a million from where I was sitting, and I leapt up and punched the air in triumph before I could restrain myself. I stole a glance at the glass doors as if expecting God to be standing there shaking his head at this loss of control, but it was too dark outside to see anything for certain. Somebody, not the Lord obviously, might have been watching me from the gloom: a stray senior lecturer maybe, wandering the campus and spying through the curtains of the lodge like a poet in search of desire. Nevertheless, it didn't matter – no one was around. I sat back at the table, feeling oddly uncomfortable about the way my legs were angled. Who had sat here before? I wondered, bouncing a little on the burgundy cushion as though there might be something in its propulsion that my arse might divine in way of an answer.

What a strange thing to do, I decided, and besides: was that the best question I could come up with? I had to ask myself: is that the sort of query Maurice Blanchot would ponder were he caught alone at night in a Parisian tavern? His name made its way into the mix of my thoughts because one of his books was in the lodge, slumped to the side of the library shelf, apparently recently read. Taking the book's displacement as a hint of its quality, I had read the first pages – something about a stranger who wanders into the city and is held indefinitely in detention for his own happiness and the sake of the people. The story was ruined by the local atmosphere of the country, where such questions came too shamefully close to the bone. Instead of enjoying the spare prose, I made creative writing critiques in the margins: 'more detail needed – we don't get much description of the protagonist's physicality, and there is little to no specificity regarding the setting – without these things it is hard to connect with the story'. It gave me great pleasure to correct a famous Frenchman.

Eventually, my phone charged and the sun rose and, just as I started to doze in my chair, it seemed suddenly to be time to go and give the lecture. I wandered along a duck-dotted path that wound its way into the campus amidst the lively chatter of students swarming the university in the cool morning air, their hands in pockets and chins tucked into scarves. I followed the directions Dani had sent me to a large lecture room. A fat man with thinning hair on his round head was standing behind the lectern, in front of a huge wall onto which a computer desktop image of an

Appalachian mountain was projected. He greeted me with a meaty handshake. His name was Damien, and he informed me, with his eyes squeezed in a fierce welcome, that he'd read and loved *A Dozen Doorbells*.

'Where's Dani?' I asked.

Damien frowned and his jowls dropped down from his jaw. 'Oh! Professor Herrick is on a residency in Paris! I apologise if that wasn't clear – but to be honest, I was the one who asked her to invite you. I think *A Dozen Doorbells on the House of Time* is a masterpiece – a total inversion of the Australian voice! It is not, as it happens, completely unlike some of my own work! I'm very pleased to have you here... Anyway, I'll tell you all my thoughts afterwards; here come the students – they've all read your book too you know!'

Damien eased into his front-row seat and winked at me, smiling openly while the room filled with young people and their mumbled morning chatter. The persistent interjection of the lecture-room door opening and slamming shut gave the students' muttered exchanges a savage punctuation. The talk was titled *Writing the Sub-City*, and I intended to show them an extract from Antigone Kefala's *Sydney Journals* in order to demonstrate to Dani that I had moved away from Henry Miller. I needed her to know that I was no longer obsessed with erections made of lead and the ghosts that are lost on university campuses.

The students shrugged through the hour and shifted in their seats. To make matters worse, I had left my copy of Kefala's *Journals* back in the lodge, and I said so to them aloud, like this: 'I'd like to draw your attention to...something I've left back at the apartment!' I thought it would make at least some of them snicker to say it that way, but I heard nothing except my finger smacking the microphone stand when I turned back to the slideshow on the lectern computer.

In her journals, I explained to the furrowed brows on the bright white faces, Kefala says that when she first came out of Europe she and her friends suffered from the lack of historical weight in the air and water, along the streets of the city, and in the cemeteries with their milky white accoutrements through which strong winds were always blowing and the pool-blue sky seemed so garish and indifferent to elemental human life. Growing older, I told them, as Kefala grows too, I begin to see how archaic a vision she was sketching. Then again, I admitted, in this new century, that I barely recognise, with its inverted myths of slouch-hatted soldiers, their ghostly images projected onto the Harbour Bridge at night, or slung in laser-light upon the sepulchral curves of the Opera House – with the Light Horsemen eternally staked into the earth between the crossed legs of the colossal motorways paved over the arse of the western suburbs – it would be hard to argue with the high tone Kefala takes, and all her perceptions of emptiness. Beside Damien, whose jowl flexed and shook its way through the talk, more attentive to my voice than its owner I thought, who held his hand up to tap at the bum of his chin on occasion, his tight eyes darting over everything in the room, there was an empty seat. If Dani were not in Paris, I supposed as I read from my notes, she would be sitting in that seat. If she were here her long curls, I realised, would be the only golden element in the botched hermeneutics of the lecture room.

'If you lose the flow of your story, your setting, your characters, for even a moment – it's all gone and you've fucked it!' I said. They shifted, listless in their seats, with a thousand pantomimes of indifference all upon me at once. Death was in their youthful gaze.

Later, back in the conference room with my board of the dead, I tossed a second dart. Unbelievable! I said with wide eyes. Another bullseye! This time it was the one with the blue fin, like a swordfish. It was stuck into the red centre of the board perfectly alongside the earlier miracle – the two darts suddenly appearing like lovers. No celebration this time: just a disembodied smile. In the dark windows of the room I saw the expression's glow reflected back at me. It was only a faint reflection on the surface of the glass, and now only a memory, but what a lonely smile it was.

DREAMS IN THE DAYLIGHT COUNTRY

1.

To try and read strange writing, signifies that you will escape enemies only by making no new speculation after this dream.
GUSTAVUS HINDMAN MILLER

This is how one becomes, through dreams, the perfect autodidact. The dream itself might not be much chop, but then, my fiction is so short that I can dine out on even the briefest, vaguest visions for an entire book. It might not be a particularly interesting dream either – but then, the audience for Australian short fiction is so slim that getting to know the desires of readers is, for me at any rate, something of a waste of time. Besides, what kind of writer concerns themselves with what the reader wants? Not a very interesting one. For interesting writers, the relationship between reader and writer is pure 'sub and dom'. The writer commands, the reader obeys. William S. Burroughs once said that teaching 'writing' was like 'trying to teach someone how to dream'. I suspect he had it right in a sense: if you cannot dream – in one form or another – then don't bother writing at all. Perhaps those with pretensions of teaching fiction to the young and the restless should be more concerned with the ethereal realms than they seem to be at present. Politics and imagination are overlapping magisteria – each realm need not be addressed in the absence of the other – but it appears to me that the literature most in production in this troubled country is a little too beholden to its own seriousness, and far too down to earth. The rabid effacement that commercialisation demands of the humanities in our higher education institutions is one destructive factor – a 'community arts' culture that seeks to trade on the commodification of every aspect of the 'writer's life' and reduces literature to an economy of gossip is another. But there is plenty of blame to go around.

In the introduction to *Cultural Amnesia* – a collection of essays derided for its self-indulgence and its many ego-maniacal liberties – Clive James, that shamefully unabashed Australian polymath, writes:

> We could, if we wished, do without remembering, and gain all the advantages of travelling light; but a deep instinct, not very different from love, reminds us that efficiency would be bought at the cost of emptiness. Finally the reason we go on thinking is because of a feeling. We have to keep that feeling pure if we can, and, if we ever lose it, try to get it back.

These words are with me almost every day. There is an air of dreamlessness – a thick, thoughtless sleep – in the atmosphere, as if our collective meetings with the unconscious have become narrowed to a cinematic aperture cliché. They have been usurped from us by benign, unfeeling hands. I don't know what is worth remembering, but I know the electric feeling that is too often missing from the world when it is written on the page. The pure light comes in from here and there, like a secret whispered between friends. It is there in the feverish marginalia and the liquid monomania of Kate Middleton's *Ephemeral Waters*, in the plangent logorrhoea of PiO's *Fitzroy*, in the ectoplasmic cine-poetry meditations of Miro Bilbrough's *Being Venice*, in Holly Isemonger's necro-sexual political prose psalms, in the distended alt-text ouroboria of Oliver Mol's *Lion Attack*, and in every line of the tectonic linguistic ecologies that make up Alexis Wright's mesmerising novels. Through the dreamers in our midst, the histories and memories of the twenty-first century rise over the dim horizon like the smoke of spectral djinn, looming entities without organs and boundaries – new and ever queerer visions for tomorrow's children to follow, and forget.

2.

To dream that you are writing, foretells that you will make a mistake which will almost prove your undoing.
GUSTAVUS HINDMAN MILLER

Dr Maria Angel was the woman who taught me everything the neophyte writer need know about their subject – and she did it almost entirely through the prism of dreaming.

Under her watch, my classmates and I – all wannabe writers smuggled into higher learning by the University of Western Sydney's special program for unexceptional students – began our journey into the murk of fiction-making by allowing dreams to dominate our waking life. Our dreams became a means of unravelling and restructuring consciousness: we were told to treat them like works of fiction – experiments in style and voice – to see in the ordinary madness of our evening's fevers all the details of the daylight world transposed, disguised, deformed and renewed. We were taught that dreams can be revised and rewritten even as they occur, and that whatever enigmatic apparatus of the unconscious governs the generation of dream-images, it can be an organ easily flattered – it blooms and spreads into a wild expanse of colours, scents and feelings under the faintest attention. Certain cheeses and spices can help enhance the length and lucidity of dreams, and make them more malleable. Drugs too, of course, though these – along with the more mundane enhancements like nicotine patches worn to bed – were not recommended by Dr Angel. Alarm clocks set for midnight catch an unwary unconscious off-guard – a notebook and pen by the bedside are essential for documenting involuntary invocations before the blinding forgetfulness of morning.

Patient with our stubborn stupidities and our lack of culture, Dr Angel (compulsively scratching at her head as she lectured) gave literary supplements to the creative dream praxis with unit readers stacked to bursting with Baudelaire,

Benjamin, Freud, and Stein – incomprehensible reading for students who had until this point in their lives barely broken the spine of a book. No easy task to explain Hélène Cixous' *Dream I Tell You* to barely literate girls and boys with the empty hills of Werrington and the long blue skies stretching out for miles outside the cramped classroom's windows. Cixous said to us, 'What a delight to head off with high hopes to night's court, without any knowledge of what may happen! Where shall I be taken tonight! Into which country? Into which country of countries?' What did it mean to write of the subtle pleasures of night's court in the form of a long love letter to another famous Frenchie, when the unfiltered fullness of an Australian afternoon sun pushed the campus air-conditioners into a weaponised drone? Looking back at *Dream I Tell You* from the hindsight of another time, is it any wonder a young student might baulk at such unwavering, unapologetic self-indulgence? Who would celebrate Cixous if her writing were to emerge here and now? Isolated poets and poetry readers might still go for that sort of luxuriousness, but who else in today's climate would stand for such navel-gazing? The level of enthusiasm with which Cixous writes would rule her out of most discussions in this ever-tightening atmosphere of neo-liberal pragmatism, and the all-powerful influence of the online consensus-lords would likely find her frivolities an apolitical nonsense – though they'd hardly admit that to themselves.

Dr Angel, a survivor from an epoch less intellectually demoralised, persisted with us despite our cynicism and the cold indifference accumulating in our institutional surroundings, though she was often flushed red with the frustration of being at the outer limits of what could be explained at all. To us, majors in a subject the university was already making moves to abandon, the readings were obtuse. But then, the seriousness of being dreamy did hold a high appeal for the flighty, flaky sorts who typically make up creative-writing courses. Like Baudelaire, my dream-soaked undergraduate peers and I all had our heads in the clouds, searching absent-mindedly for the miracle of a perfect imagining – one in which the ever-changing web of consciousness that writing weaves into existence might reveal itself uniquely – and be captured with our own names on the covers.

3.

For an author to dream of his works going to press, is a dream of caution; he will have much trouble in placing them before the public.'
GUSTAVUS HINDMAN MILLER

At first I was reluctant to follow Dr Angel's command to begin recording dreams – they'd always been trouble for me, and for my lapsed-Catholic family. The whole lot of us had prophetic 'visions' – we were cursed with the satanic habit of prophesying as we tossed and turned. From an early age, Mum and I would, over tea and Weet-Bix, look through a large book titled *1001 Dreams Interpreted*, and indulge in the diabolical ritual of its occult analyses. On the cover of the book, which I still have here on the shelf – tranquilised by the weight of a children's Bible – is a crystal ball with images of random nouns (a tiger, a clip-art mouth, the Great Pyramid of Giza), adrift in the dark ether contained by the fortune teller's globe. 'To dream of sharks,' the book warns, 'portends familial discord,' whereas 'to see someone riding a bicycle' speaks of 'a desire to achieve greater balance in one's domestic and professional spheres.' It is an odd book and a blunt but useful tool, working the way fortune cards do: pricking out the threads of a narrative upon which the customer might lay their intuitions and imaginings. Ours was the behaviour of another century: the days before cable news came to town and the internet made most information instant. My mother was often fretful that the lost child she'd seen crying in her dream might be hidden in a backstreet nearby – still waiting for rescue – or that the murdered woman's body she'd spied drifting bloated down the green waters of the Georges River would go too long unnoticed to bring justice to the killer. Occasionally there was evidence that she had glimpsed an actual reality – for want of a better phrase. None of us doubted this mystical gift – or the hauntings we suffered weekly in our home. Sometimes these visitations turned violent – disruptive – and talismans (a ceramic evil eye, a gnostic gemstone) were placed about the house to keep the spirits content. My brother had the most mundane prophetic visions imaginable – occasionally glimpsing in advance the serial numbers and barcodes on shipping deliveries at the frozen-goods warehouse he worked for – a truly useless Nostradamus.

For myself, dreams were an exhausting kind of allergy that made daylight hours an effervescent bramble of thorny irritation. I was afflicted with what I have heard others call night terrors, dreams in which I lay paralysed in fright, as faceless shadow men pressed their ink-black faces against the bedroom window, their sucking lipless mouths threatening to steal me into an infernal plain so fearful, I would wake screaming and shuddering in shock and sweat, the flat, impassive eyeless glare of these devils still glowing ether-black inside my mind like bloodied vapour in the air.

These nightmare beings so filled me with a horror of sleeping that I was forced to devise a kind of mystic ritual against the night. I'd lie in bed and picture one of the demon beings hovering in the air, then I would encase him in a makeshift prison: a golden orb the size of a coffin, or a concrete tomb without windows or doors. Around that I would place another larger confinement, an immense silver dome, or some solid hemisphere of forged iron. From here I would increase the scale, the planet that this original confinement was located on would need itself to be fully contained, and that planetary encasing would then in turn need to be trapped in some colossal, intergalactic holding. Each prison would require another, greater prison, and this process would need to be endlessly repeated, prisons within prisons, interdimensional tombs inside the eyes of giants swallowed by solar storms of unfathomable ice and stone within an atom of another dimension, a solid bronze egg frozen in a diamond case larger than the immeasurable sun, and on and on, until the sky outside, in the real world, would begin to lighten, and I could pass to sleep in the safe hours between dawn and breakfast, where demons have no foothold on our earth. Should I, at any time during this generative ritual of ever-increasing imaginative feats, accidentally recall the original spectre of the demon creature in my mind's eye, then the whole exercise would fail, and I would scramble to place the escaped spirit back into a new and original restraint, or else face the villain's redoubled wrath.

I performed this complex ritual every night for many years, and I have long suspected that this activity is the reason I was drawn to the idea of writing – seduced by the promise of the redemptive recursions to be found in mental interiors. It was only once I was old enough to read unassisted that I was able to replace this tiresome practice of mental capture with the act of training my eyes on the tight hermetic lines made by sentences in the pages of books. I wandered around in the daylight, tired from my mental ablutions, in an abstracted daze – head full of the dramas of night.

Perhaps for this reason, and for the odd way I stared blankly into a void when we sat at the dinner table, my mother took me to see a psychiatrist in Liverpool. His name, as I recall it slotted on his office door, was Dr Redoyavitch. He had a short cropped, reddish beard – not unlike my stepfather's – and a wicker basket beside his desk. There were action figures stacked inside – a little Yoda, a vascular He-man, assorted professional wrestlers in their brightly coloured tights. From the games I made of these idols, Redoyavitch diagnosed me as a troubled child. I told him about my recurrent night terrors too: sometimes an enormous eye with a golden iris crashes in through the bedroom window, at other times a malignant shade burning like a black candle takes over my body – and under the influence of such recurring themes I'd lose control, could not breathe, would sweat in the sheets until I was too slippery for sleep. The doctor made notes about all this, then later dumped me as a patient and took in my mother – about whom he wrote a doctoral thesis.

Suspecting no good could come from the revival of those belligerent dreams – long since annihilated by puberty and all its excesses – I nevertheless did as Dr Angel instructed. With the high tide of post-structuralism ebbing away from the universities and creative speculation giving way to unadulterated commercialism, these lessons in dreaming staked us to something solid: Dr Angel grounded us in the deep and fecund world of imagination. My impoverished, unlettered head suddenly became, thanks to her reprogramming, a nightly avalanche of alternative ontologies – worlds within worlds all as intricate and complex as the material reality they took as their inspiration. They became the high point of existence. As Cixous suggests, the meridians of emotion in everyday life are mere footnotes to the fullest range of feeling in dream states, with their mind-bending terrors and ecstasies. There – in the revisions of the dream-breath – peoples, languages, voices, faces, cities, circumstances, gods and intimacies seemingly unthinkable to conscious labour – surge with all the ferocity of life's infinite wellspring. All universes conceivable to the human mind pass before our eyeless gaze. What this excess presented to us as young writers was an inexhaustibly royal road to forging fictions in the real world. Nothing else was necessary; the realer materials of life became a redundant source of inspiration in the light of dream's infinitudes. Lest this read like hyperbole – I will prove it through experiment.

4.

To see writing, denotes that you will be upbraided for your careless conduct and a lawsuit may cause you embarrassment.
GUSTAVUS HINDMAN MILLER

Presently, I gather up the novel closest to hand – Gerald Murnane's *A History of Books* – and proceed to the couch. It is mid-afternoon and my neighbour is imitating a dog; his barking is distinct through the cramped walls of our house on the hill. On the couch now, I observe that the white curtain on our front door lends a funereal glow to my mother, who is asleep on a chair, her figure framed by my feet on the armrest. Nothing is moving but spores of dust, drifting around us both like luminous satellites in this odd tableau of the living room. It is hot, and the neighbour continues to improve on his dog impressions. Only thirty pages into *A History of Books* I put it down – open on my chest like a broken fan. The strange image provoked by Murnane's paragraph about a paragraph – narrators without names, without faces, recurring clauses

– repeat in a numbing choral murmur as the book slides down my chest and onto my throat: already I'm at the gates of sleep.

The book presses awkwardly against my flesh and, with arms at my side, I think of something which will carry consciousness away. Here it comes: I am climbing up to the summit of a cliff somewhere on a cool spring afternoon. A hand-hold of weed growing from a crack in a smooth rock near a lighthouse helps me to make the final steps upwards – reveals the coastal vista. Being there with family – brother, wife, one of my fathers: putting our different hands up on the steel fence to look out over the view. The long, trembling, ink-blue water to the east stretches into a cuticle-white horizon. I wonder if there is something to the strained feeling of anticipation when looking down the cliff at the sea against the outcrops rimmed round the shore. Waves in collision recede to foam. The strangely alien beach vegetation and its dry shrubs bristle at our feet in the altitude's breeze. The lighthouse is a sandstone ruin, the great grey bricks are piled at the round base like spilt entrails, and the hollow remains are fenced to keep the tourists from climbing through the cracks. A wooden signpost complete with pictures of ghostly families, centuries dead, tells us the lighthouse was built incorrectly – without consulting the maritime authorities – its deceptive light leading ships to wreck on the jagged coastline. The keeper's son fell from the cliff in 1896. A daughter accidentally shot. Another's throat slit from 'ear to ear'. I pretend I am looking for a whale, away from my family, not mesmerised by history, sea or sky but by expectation – an almost imperceptible sense of impending disappointment, as if the constant ebb and rush of the waves is always holding back its drowned and swallowed secrets. A long way out, the surface breaks with froth, and a hint of finned black immensity rolls above the water. The sight of that salty mammalian hide reminds me of a dream I had before my wedding night: alone in a boat on a green-grey evening – lopping over the rolling waters with the clank of oars in their sockets and my body slick with sea-spray and sweat. From underneath came the surge of a colossal black whale, its enormous head rising beside me like a sudden tidal eclipse. The open maw was lined with waxen teeth, and a tongueless throat leading into its cavernous pink gut began to suck in the sea, while the sound of a gargantuan gurgling rang, until the vision ended with my waking. Later, talking with a friend on the green lawn of Sydney University's campus with the midday sun on our pale skin like hot grease, she told me that whales signified feminine destructive energy. Now, back at the lighthouse, the (real) whale does not resurface. I can't be sure it was ever there, and at the height of this uncertainty, the dream loses its colour, and then sinks into an infinite darkness.

5.

To dream of old books, is a warning to shun evil in any form.
GUSTAVUS HINDMAN MILLER

From the black depths of one dream's dissolution another has arisen, revealing itself to me in a foggy order, beginning with a climb up a staircase beneath Haymarket Library. At its summit I find myself standing in a room of the library where the walls glow a Martian red. About me, filling the square shape of the room, is a crowd of young people facing a stage upon which, beneath a great stained-glass window, a celebrated man, whose face I cannot quite make out, is speaking with sonorous tones into a microphone. The crowd of young people are frozen in rapture, grinning in wonder at the figure on the stage as he speaks. I too wish to be rapt, and strain to hear from the back of room what words of wisdom this storyteller is speaking, but just as I begin to focus on his speech, a poet from Parramatta named Peter, whose hair is long and whose fingers are covered in biker rings, accosts me at the threshold of the crowd. His face, like the walls and shelves around us in the small, square room, is bathed in the strange red light, and his eyes are wide open, but he alone seems unabsorbed by the talk of the man upon the stage. To my great astonishment, Peter the poet begins excitedly, loudly, to explain that he has discovered, through sheer force of logic, the absolute truth. 'The universe cannot be,' Peter earnestly entreats me, his ringed fingers wriggling in excitement as he speaks, 'the result of anything external to it, since anything which can affect the contents of our universe in even the most infinitesimal way must logically correspond to a component of it, which implies that only that which is within the given horizons of our reality can observe it, since observation is itself an act of determination, and if that is the case, as logic asserts it must surely be, then the universe we inhabit is, in every dimension and in the final analysis, a matter of the purest self-definition. That is to say, it is a place of absolute freedom, indeed, it is the very essence of freedom, the only possible manifestation of freedom, since it lies irrefutably unrestrained by any logically permissible external agency!'

Peter the poet speaks so loudly and the proximity of his mouth to my face is such that it proves impossible to hear the words of the famous figure who is speechifying on the stage. I look around for support from someone nearby in the crowd, thinking they too must find the poet's exhortations the height of rudeness, but so entranced are all about us with pleasure at whatever it is they are hearing that no one seems to notice the poet's shrill incivility. I try politely to push my way through the throng to escape him as he continues talking, but he follows along, saying, 'It will perhaps, at first, seem to you that I have overdetermined the power of logic in subjugating the universe itself to such a constraint, but it is untenable to suppose that the universe itself is a place of chaos and irrationality. A simple thought experiment might easily reveal this is so. Our reality, in which logical formulation is possible, is one in which language, which is itself a form of logic, is born from the sheer power of our universe's natural law. Language is the nature of the universe, a place of tautological self-definition in action.'

I snake onward towards the stage. The young people around me are all so tall I soon get lost between their shoulders as I shove politely forward. Disoriented, I emerge from the crowd on the far side of the room, near the shelves and adjacent to the stage. There, I discover the source of the red glow in the room is a blindingly bright fire, slowly spreading from book to book like a molten serpent slithering across their spines. I turn to the young people closest to me, wondering how they have failed to comprehend the intense heat and the golden-red glow of the burning books. I grab at a young woman beside me with one hand, pointing wordlessly at the blaze with the other like a character in a child's cartoon who has seen a ghost and yet cannot bring himself to speak. But the young woman will not be turned.

Realising how entranced the young people are, I begin to grab at their clothes. When this fails to break their focus I resorted to clawing at their faces with my nails and to kick at their shins with my steel-cap boots, to scream in their ears with all my will. When that has no effect, I start to argue with them, then merely to insult, to call them selfish and stupid. I try to incite them with ever greater insults, call them racists and bigots and cowards, but this too has no effect. I succumb to fury, start to punch them, I strike the back of their heads, their mouths and kidneys, but my arms move as if underwater. What's worse, I can still hear Peter the poet talking, and he is saying, 'Once we accept these basic axioms of the universe as a place of sheer, self-defining meaning, it is only logical that we are empowered to conceive of ourselves as the highest approximations of the mind of God – whose pantheistic presence is manifestly demonstrated by the extension of this arithmetic – there is, therefore, an absolute truth shining out from the beating red heart of existence.' Now, beyond desperate to save the crowd from the threat of immolation, I plunge my hands into their pants and tights and jiggle and pluck at their genitals, and I bite the skin of their necks, but still they will not notice me or the fire around us, and I sob and cry and at last when the smoke makes me cough and choke, and I begin to smell an awful burning stench, I drop to the floor. There, through their unmovable legs, I crawl towards the stairs, and roll down them in a desperate fall as the heat pushes at my back and licks my limbs with sudden ferocity.

Outside in the cold street I look up at the stained-glass window and watch the flames dancing, thinking of the young people being incinerated inside. Through the coloured glass the red and yellow of the fire spreads a halo of blue and green out into the deserted Sydney night, while the walls of the library smoke and I can feel the pulse of steam hissing through the body of the building. Peter puts his ringed hand on my shoulder, having apparently escaped with me, though his hair is singed and smouldering, and his face is covered in soot like someone in a children's movie who has played with fire and been scorched. When he speaks his manner seems tempered, as if the harshness of the inferno has burned out his mania.

'The Hebrews,' he says, 'have a story about Joseph that always makes me laugh. He finds himself in an Egyptian prison, and there he comes upon a royal baker and a carpenter. "Why do you guys look so miserable?" he says. "Because," the carpenter tells him, "there's nobody about to read our dreams." So Joseph gives them a look at his technicolour coat and says, "Give me your dreams, and I'll have a word to God". The baker goes first, and says, "Every night I dream of seven balls of dough rolling down a hill, I chase after them, but they go in seven different directions, and I end up empty-handed." Joseph furrows his brow for a bit and says "Good news! I've asked God and your dream means that seven days from now the Pharaoh will have a change of heart and you'll be invited back to the palace." "Oh God thou art merciful!" the baker cries, and falls to the floor of the prison and kisses Joseph's feet in joy. The carpenter is overjoyed too, on hearing this revelation, because his dream is almost identical to the baker's, only it's seven logs in his that go rolling down the hill, and take seven different paths, and so he leaps to his feet and says to Joseph, "Quick, do me next!" Joseph listens to this virtually identical dream, furrows his brow again and says, "God says Pharaoh is going to crucify you and your family in the centre of town."' Peter takes his ringed hand from my shoulder, wipes a smear of soot from his face and says, 'Always makes me laugh, that does,' as the two of us watch the auroral arrangement of reds and blues and greens glimmering in the dark.

The colour fades, and my eyes open. The dream is over, and back in the daylight world, things remain as ordinary as ever. The neighbour has ceased his barking. I can hear him knocking now – a hammer against the wall. That man is always doing three or more things at once. Talking to his son now, between swings, then his wife. What is he saying? Car boots are being slammed outside in the street. It must be time for church, and the slow parade of ancient people on their way to service will be coming down the footpath. My eyes are tired and my mother has left the frame. There is no one in the house, and the smell of smoke from the barbecue next door wafts through the open window, the rich scent of charring meat and coal. For a moment the shock of the real makes it hard to recall what I've just seen in my sleep, but, thread by thread, I pull it back into mind, and move to the table to write it down.

THE CULT OF WESTERN SYDNEY

There were six of us facing the director in the backstage area, far enough away from the curtain closed across the stage of the Bankstown theatre to keep our nerves in check. The theatre itself was a recently opened building, a local council triumph of tall glass perimeters, stainless steel handrails, and an elegantly minimalist architectural blandness. They'd named the place in honour of an actor who'd made it in Hollywood in the eighties and was now, in the eyes of the Sydney arts community, the suburb's strongest case for artistic and cultural relevance, though few who passed beneath the grand transparent doors would recognise his face or the titles of his films with great accuracy. Our stage director, a short thin woman with dark close-cropped hair – well known for bringing an experimental type of theatre to Australian shores – was walking us through a series of exercises intended to hone our plosives, sharpen our fricatives, and counter the deadening effect of our collective tendency to mispronunciation, so that the opening night's performances would be as fluent and nuanced as we'd all rehearsed them to be. At her instruction, we flicked our tongues against clenched teeth, popped our puffed-up mouths in a flatulent manner, and pretended to yawn till our jaws ached with repeated over-extension. These drills were then topped off with an intense regime of tongue twisters, all of us repeating 'selfish shellfish', 'she sells sea shells', 'a big black bear sat on a big black rug' and 'six sleek swans swam swiftly southwards' to the point of semantic discombobulation.

We'd been told to expect a full house in the hall that evening; the Sydney Writers' Festival had included our 'performance reading' in its vast catalogue of literary events as part of its 'way out west' outreach program. Reminded of this fact, the more politically savvy amongst our crew began to grumble that we ought to have been invited east like the rest of the writers on the festival program, adding that it was a predictable demonstration of the hierarchical behaviour of a white, middle-class institution. Thinking on this, another member of the group added that it was patronising to marginalised groups to deploy terminology like 'special programs' and 'outreach', especially when the real agenda of the festival was clearly to co-opt our crew's diversity and dilute the subversive nature of our writing without allowing it to disrupt the seamless veneer of faux-inclusivity that characterised the Australian literary world. Were anyone to counter that we were lucky to be asked to be part of an internationally recognised writers' festival when none of us had ever actually published anything, the obvious rejoinder would have been that if Australian publishing was focused on the potential of up-and-coming talents – especially those in marginalised and oppressed communities – rather than those white-bread authors whose appeal is limited to an ageing middle-class population, then perhaps more of us would have been able to publish books of our own. This analysis was augmented by another member of the crew, who scoffed that it was evidence of the dehumanising and adversarial extent of late capitalism's toxicity that our status as 'bookable' artists was determined by having our names attached to a commercial product.

The director interrupted this discussion to take us through the final exercise, where we were asked to close our eyes and envision the sun setting over a tropical beach at dusk, raising our arms slowly as we inhaled a deep, slow, soothing breath, and then – luxuriating momentarily in our calm fullness – we were to exhale, gracefully letting our arms float down to our sides like feathers moving through thick air. We were each asked to repeat this meditation three times in slow succession, our stage director encouraging us to keep our eyes closed to guard our attention against the growing intensity of the arriving audience, whose presence was unmistakably audible as they made their creaking way into the auditorium's seating area, the growing background noise of their excited chatter pushing in at us through the winding corridor's crisp acoustics and carrying with it an irresistible contagion of ecstatic terror. It was a struggle to keep the eyes closed against the thought of the faces accumulating before the stage we were moments from stepping up onto, but I managed to hold myself in the thrall of the meditation by substituting the mental picture of some vague tropical beach with the familiar view of the skyline from my home in Mt Pritchard, where great ash-green ghost gums swayed in a burly wind, and on the horizon, the sight of Centrepoint Tower was a spindle of steel the size and shape of a turntable needle.

It occurred to me – eyes tight, the image of my childhood background bright and blue in my mind – that because it was now late in the evening, the tip of the tower would be flashing an electric violet light, like the first lick of flame from a birthday candle, which would be just discernible from the back windows of our house. This view of the city on the horizon had been the ever-present background scenery of my life, the entirety of which had been orientated by the distance between the landmark of the tower – made miniature for us outside the window – and my suburban existence of Colorbond-bound yards with dried-out lawns on which utes, trucks, and swing sets sank into the climbing weeds and the Hills Hoists tilted their grey skeletal limbs towards the earth. The scene pinned my life into place, not least because the Centrepoint building happened to contain the office where my father worked. Home from school I'd stand by the window in my blue uniform, contemplating the thin sliver of the tower on the edge of the visible world with a melancholy of familial longing – wondering how the bustle of the city was treating my dad: his black suitcase and polished shoes, his starched white shirts, the black hairs furling down from his beard onto his collar, the tensed plane of his squared shoulders and his rolled sleeves when he went marching, at the end of the day, from out of the immense building at the city's centre and into the thrumming life of the streets with a lit cigarette on his lips. If I closed my eyes by the open window of the house and pressed the top of my nose against the flyscreen I could almost smell that distinct sweet odour of his sweat and the trace of smoke and coffee that permeated his tanned skin. At seven in the evening, when the clocks of the house would chime and my stepdad would settle down to watch deranged neighbours feuding over fences on *A Current Affair*, and the sun was starting to sink behind our hill, I'd sometimes imagine my father leaving the British-Ex where he used to drink, catching the train west to his home several suburbs away from ours, wondering what expression he had on his face while the world of skyscrapers and suits gave ground to the low and level fibro of the suburbs. Despite working in the city's tallest building, the immutable logic of geography meant my dad could not see our place, even if he went out onto the tourist section of the tower and dropped coins into the telescopic binoculars on the outer rims of the structure's enormous head. If he ever stood in the treacherous winds out on the deck and looked to the west and scanned for us in the plains of fibro homes with above-ground pools and trampolines in their yards, he never said so to me.

All these impressions went with me up the stairs and onto the Bankstown theatre's stage, but when the velvet curtain came up and we were immersed in the collective energies of the audience whose faces were obscured by the ferocity of the spotlights aimed at us, all thought of the past was obliterated. We were perched on thin stools with microphones angled at our faces, and our stories were printed in the form of booklets and placed on music stands at arm's length. We were supposed to follow along as each member of the ensemble read, turning the pages of the script in unison so that no one would be out of place or miss their cue. I listened to the readings of the other writers go by, their voices rolling over the sentences and exclamations I'd heard a thousand times in our rehearsals, sweat running down my temples and pouring from my armpits. The idea that in a matter of moments it would be my voice passing through the amplification system and out into the brutal mix of blinding lights and darkened faces in the hall sparked through my nerves like an electric scream that lasted right up until the story before mine ended and the dreaded cue to begin reading arrived like the fall of a guillotine blade. The internal apoplexy of screaming nerves leapt up and took possession of my mouth, which moved through the motions and made the approximate sounds the words on the page were supposed to represent at a rapidity and volume far exceeding what I had intended. I read so quickly and maniacally that the whole thing was over in a burst of nervous seconds, and the instant the last sentence had been spoken my body slumped into a post-adrenaline delirium during which the only thing that kept me erect in the stool was the collective force of the crowd's thousand invisible eyes.

After a few more readings the event was over. An applause rose up from the crowd, and we were sent out down the stage's stairs and into the audience by our director, who gave us a beaming smile with her perfect teeth and touched our shoulders as we went by on our way to meet what she was calling with earnestness 'our new fans'. With the lights on I could make out my mum and my brother in a centre row, and I waved at them so they'd know it was okay to leave. They smiled back, looking a mixture of proud and uncertain, my mother's deep blue eyes and my brother's lips tensely pursed, revealing that concealed contradiction of affection and mistrust he carried with him everywhere in those years. While my family was waving themselves outside, a diminutive ageing actor, whose decades-long career consisted of having his scenes cut from some of Australia's finest films, shook my hand and announced with a sardonic smirk, 'I really enjoyed the way you read. I was laughing the whole way through.' I thanked him, but he held onto my hand and added, 'Was I supposed to be laughing though? Cause I really wasn't sure if you're just like that?' I thanked him again, not sure what else to say and he laughed. I went out to lean on the stainless steel in the lobby and be away from the crowd, which was hurrying towards the hall's glass doors. A rotund gentleman in a Grateful Dead shirt under a suit-jacket snuck up behind me. He had one arm tucked firmly around the waist of a tall, bosomy woman who seemed determined to look over her shoulder and out of the lobby at something happening in the darkness, her long hair tumbling around the man's shoulder as if attempting to grasp his enormous throat in a noose of locks. 'You mentioned Nietzsche in your reading,' he said. 'But what of his have you read?' I put my hands in my pockets and attempted to list the little of Nietzsche's back-catalogue I'd managed to slog my way through, but his companion interrupted, saying 'He's read his name somewhere so he regurgitated it in his stories,' and flashed him a wide-eyed look as if desperately begging to cut short a tedious subject and leave the scene. 'Is that right?' he asked, his eyes narrowing and his fingers sliding down into his shirt so that the hairs on his pale chest were visible. Then he coughed loudly and said, 'Well aren't you a little moron then!' just as his wife managed to pull him away so he was free to walk out through the tall glass sliding doors and into the night.

After several encounters like these, including one in which an elderly woman thanked me for representing the travails of Asperger's syndrome sufferers so courageously, the crew regrouped in the backstage area, our smudged scripts tucked into our pockets or stuffed into handbags or tossed into the theatre's bins. The night, our first public performance as a group, was deemed an unequivocal triumph by those whose voices mattered most. The more vocal members of our group were certain that the audience who had come to the Bankstown theatre that evening would never forget what they'd witnessed. Were any one of us slow enough on the uptake to question what it was that the attendees had seen or heard in the hall that they might be inclined to retain longer than a week or two, thorough expositions by one of our more perspicacious members could easily be provided to demonstrate the uniqueness of the writing that our collective had read aloud on the stage. Since none of us had been published before, the spokesperson might say, there was no way anyone in the audience could have experienced writing like ours. What we represented as a collective was not merely another group of unknown artists – we were the manifestation of a new literary movement from the margins of a society that was debased by its domination under a malignant white supremacist, capitalist, patriarchal status quo. This unspoken case was persuasive, and I suspect it was in the dim gloom of the Bankstown theatre's backstage area, laughing and sighing in the relief of having made it through our readings without much error, drenched in sweat and high on the vestigial electricity of having performed our work for the reward of applause, that the seed of an insidious grandeur began to flow from the vainest members of our collective and into the general heart of our Western Sydney writing group.

Despite acquiring a newfound sense of our own gravitas, many of the members of the group had a hard time committing words to the page, and our momentum stalled. Slaves as we were to the barbaric necessities of a capitalist economy, many of us were too worn down by menial jobs in call centres, bowling clubs, or working as checkout chicks in shopping centres to actually do any writing. New, more disciplined members were sought to increase the group's productivity, and regular workshops were established so that we could keep track of one another and encourage slower members to keep the production line of poetry and prose flowing. These workshops were not the usual writers' group meeting where a bunch of ineffectual hobbyists massage each other's egos and smother one another in vague platitudes – they were adversarial and caustic events, a place where sloppiness and inattention were considered intolerable. Because our duty to represent a new and radical movement in Australian letters was so immensely serious, it was necessary that the work we produced was flawless. As it happened, much of the work our members brought to the workshops was under-cooked, over-written, full of erroneous grammatical eccentricities, and, most egregiously, the drafts our members produced were often at odds with the political aesthetic that our more senior members were committed to fomenting. The intensity of the workshops was an essential means of correcting these deviations from our collective, and a chance for those of us who knew most about everything to lend their knowledge to those who knew close to nothing at all.

One of our leading members, through careful consideration of the Western canon as an undergrad, had discovered that the central distinguishing factor between high literature and mere writing was the philosophical abstraction of 'showing' rather than 'telling'. To come to terms with this complex technical concept, the workshops often required a breaking down of the failings and weaknesses of the writer to their roots – the inadequacies of their work were often connected to their misconceptions of the world around them – and then the rebuilding of this writer from the ground up, into a more morally and ethically vigorous person whose writing would inevitably be improved by the intervention. Our learned comrades assisted many such writers by suggesting to them what verbs, nouns, clauses and subject matters might best fill the gaps in their simplistic sketches of human experience, taking it upon themselves to act as arbiters of what might serve as appropriate subject matter for literary endeavour.

The effect of these workshops, and the wise counsel of our more learned members, was that the group's writing improved, and our short stories found publication in all the journals and literary rags around town. The arts organisation which housed and auspiced our activities occupied a series of cramped offices across from the railway station to begin with, but they and several other local organisations managed to lobby for the money to create a brand new building, one which had its own theatre space, and soon enough we had found ourselves a comfortable and fitting base of operations. It was whispered by some of our more intuitive members that the real reason government bureaucrats had consented to the construction of the new building was that even amongst the crusty halls of the state government, people were talking about the work we were accomplishing out in the Western Suburbs. We published this 'work' in journals of our own making, and we held grand launches and 'performance readings' every few months, filling the new theatre of the arts centre with hundreds of people – mostly family and friends – on every occasion. This accumulating success was financed by a steady stream of funding applications that our senior members were perpetually writing. I remember being amazed that the government was willing to give tens of thousands of dollars to us to write stories and publish books, to launch them and promote them, and I was relieved that none of this money was in my own name – the finance side of things was always handled by the more senior members of the organisation, people who could be trusted with the paperwork.

To build a brand is no easy task, and our leading members did their utmost to make our collective presence known. Inflamed by the passion that comes from taking on a noble cause, they became powerhouses of self-promotion – and every individual in the group was a node in this nexus of name recognition. If one of our number found themselves published somewhere, all of us benefitted from the exposure. When enough blogs and journals and anthologies had been conquered, we set our collective sights on single-author publications – which is of course the goal of every aspiring writer. A local publishing house with an interest in 'unique voices' and young writers came calling, and some of our members were snatched up into that dreamy glory of having a book to call one's own. Before the first manuscripts were ready for the printers, it was decided by our leading members that the arts centre was insufficient to house our collective aspirations or our expanding numbers. Now that our members were about to have their own collections and novels published and launched and read and reviewed, it was logical that they would be offered spots at festivals and to speak at universities across the country – perhaps overseas, given time. According to our more globally minded members, it was essential for the dignity of the collective that we leave behind our current accommodations at the arts centre and find new digs that might provide a more fitting setting for writers of our burgeoning status. We relocated to the local university campus, where we were surrounded by professors and scholars – a milieu more appropriate for our growing eminence.

Not long after we moved, it was revealed by our senior members that the arts centre which had formerly housed us was not only insufficient to contain our ambitions, but also irredeemably corrupt. Though none of us had noticed at the time, the centre which had so recently been our residence was in fact a place degraded by its conformity to the structural inequalities of white supremacist culture. Were any of us shocked by this revelation, and asked for an example of its iniquity, one of the more clear-eyed members of the group would have pointed out that despite being in a culturally diverse suburb, the centre was run by an older white male, who had failed to pass on the cultural capital he had accrued over decades of service in an ethnically diverse region. Pushed on this topic, the clear-eyed members of the group might have professed that they were personally offended that the manager of this organisation had failed to surrender his job to someone more representative of the community – one of our senior members for instance. But for any one of us to have been shocked by the venal corruption of the arts centre would have been uncharacteristic of our group at the time – the workshopping we'd been committed to had not only sharpened our writing, it had honed our minds to the point that we all seemed to be in agreement on almost everything, especially those subjects which our learned members were most vocal about, and so if it was proclaimed that an organisation or a person was unsavoury, we found ourselves agreeing so vehemently, it was difficult to imagine we hadn't been the ones to think of it first.

Had any of us spoken up to disavow the cunning prophecies and promises of our growing collective ego on the night of our debut theatre reading, it might have made a difference, but by the time we had taken up our new lodgings, the loudest and proudest amongst our crew could crush any dissent by scowling and pointing to the reviews and articles by local scholars and the self-proclaimed authorities in the literary scene that concurred with our most grandiose self-promotions. There was no denying, the true-believing Western Sydney writer might have explained, that there was something unique about the literature coming from our members' books and collections, because just such exclamations were coming from tastemakers on the subject. So enthusiastic were the reviews and citations of the group's readings and publications that it became commonplace for certain literary types to suggest that Australia's literary 'centre' appeared to be shifting – or leaning, at the least – towards Sydney's 'suburban frontier'. When this declaration became a familiar refrain, and caused much discussion in our crew on how best to perpetuate this change of centre, a festival director with an ear for the tremors of his aspirational allies proclaimed that 'Western Sydney is the capital of Australian literature...if not already, then certainly it's the future,' and we took his words as granted by the time he offered them. Were any of us struck by a cynical mood of doubt, unswayed perhaps by the authority of local literary figures, whose manna was exuberant generosity and casual sycophancy, then serious critics, who were suddenly on record as suffering the same illusions, might be cited as evidence against the stubborn irrationality of doubting our mutual destiny. Slam poetry champions, Miles Franklin winners, renowned literary critics and senior academics were all apparently under the impression that our crew of writers constituted an 'important moment in Australian culture'.

Drunk on our own publicity and self-importance, we made the decision to strengthen our claim to whatever seriousness of status was bound to come our way by rebranding ourselves as literary militants. There were frequent fantasies of explosive behaviour amongst the collective, and many of us now wore a uniform, black with matching berets and bonds tops, and we arrived at festival events in enough numbers to take up entire rows of chairs, sitting up front to keep grim, stony-faced sentry over panels and lectures on topics we deemed worthy of our attention, where we would demand answers to questions about the whiteness of the authors who were presenting, or make sly accusations about cultural appropriation and the implicit immorality of those who didn't really seem like allies in our crusade to rearrange the landscape of Australian literature. On the subject of the publishing 'scene' our members began to speak with the slogans of Malcom X, as if there was some righteous necessity that we were driven by which justified an open hostility towards anyone who distracted attention from our ascendency. When one of our members spoke at an event, we applauded their every emphasis – when they were offstage, we huddled and cross-checked the status of our loyalties and certitudes, who in the room could be trusted and who declared an enemy. It became common to hear our members remark that 'we were the only ones doing anything interesting with language in the country'. Were anyone to raise an eyebrow at this statement and ask, with all respect, what it was exactly that we were doing with language, a torrent of explication would pour forth, explaining to the unbeliever that having been born into a country that celebrates its red-dusted sweeping plains and the curves of our sun-swept coasts, we in the Western Suburbs had suffered the almost gothic indignity of being pinned to the more mythologised provinces of the country, and now that this tectonic cultural movement was ready to erupt into an explosion of artistic force, we – a select few writers who happened to have come along at precisely the right time – were to be this literary reformation's winged heralds. Through us and our fictions and poems, the ten percent of the nation's population whose lives had come and gone without the alchemical touch of literary attention – the generations of people who had toiled thanklessly in the recesses of the Western Suburbs – would be given a voice, and it would be the whirling, tempestuous voice of the marginalised and oppressed, not least because our crew rightfully represented the full intersectional spectrum of Australia's downtrodden and disenfranchised. We were the Suburban Avengers. Where the figure of the 'westie' had long been reduced to a vague parade of threadbare stereotypes – bong-smoking bogans drinking longnecks in 'Penriff'; dragon-tattooed heroin dealers from Cabra; bikie gangsters of middle-eastern appearance doing drive-bys through the streets of Bankstown – the new 'westie spring' of Australian literature would sweep through the culture, knocking these caricatures aside and leaving emancipatory nuances in our wake.

Government funding for the arts poured into our collective's coffers at the sound of these rhetorical pronouncements, and we brought our radical ideas about literature to bemused school kids on the tax-payers' dime. From the classrooms we plucked out and converted young people with an interest in the arts, and did the same at arts organisations, greedy for new believers to swell our peripheral ranks. Our movement adopted a name, a logo, and a strict top-down hierarchy. It was decided at a meeting of our senior members that there would be one leader, self-appointed, and all other loyal members would be given the subordinate rank of associates. Troublesome and unruly writers who disagreed too often at meetings, or slowed the progress of the movement with their stupidities, or demonstrated a stubborn inability to adopt the correct attitudes towards our goals and targets, were disowned and disgraced. At subsequent meetings their inadequacies were dissected at great length, and the group would spend many hours bemoaning the strain that those wayward members had always caused the group and its effectiveness, though we had often failed to notice how much of a drag they had been until after they became dismembered. One of the first writers who was thrown out of our collective replied via email that he hoped our leader succeeded in finding the 'compliant group of writers he was obviously looking for', and we discussed the absurdity of this cruel and fatuous implication at our next meeting, all of us agreeing that the fact that our ex-comrade could describe us as compliant conformists rather than recognise the radical and critical nature of our group was a startling reflection of his inability to comprehend the necessity of the collective's cohesion in accomplishing the great tasks we envisioned for ourselves.

Were anyone in our midst to stop and question the rightness of our consensus on this subject, they would inevitably have to join the ranks of the excommunicated and be reduced to the pitiful position of watching from the outside how eager journalists, literary figures, arts organisations and community leaders were to confirm our self-belief and sing the collective's praises as a group of important radicals. Swathes of radio interviews, newspaper articles and television sound bites favourable to our stated mission demonstrated how profoundly ready the culture was for the great task of bringing the Western Suburbs to voice through our growing programs of workshops, publications and events. It became clear to us that the degree to which arts brokers feted our movement was an unfailing indication as to where they sat on the spectrum of moral righteousness – those who disagreed with us, who stormed out of our members' panel talks or refused to invite us to their events – were invariably on the wrong side of history. On the other hand it seemed unerringly to be the case that those who affirmed our every move and supported our every action without question were useful, but naïve, and so we were forced to deduce that the only people who had any purchase on the virtuous side of the culture was the collective itself, and even there it appeared that, amongst our own ranks, it was our leader who most exemplified the ideals we championed of our own free will.

When the Writers' Festival line-up was released each year, we were not only a permanent part of the program, but our attendance was requested at the rich end of town, given full-colour exposure in the promotional brochures and featured prominently in the press for the event itself – though not as prominently as we felt was fitting for our status in the literary scene. At the program launches we scoffed at their canapes and champagne, though we were given permission to eat and drink them. Speeches were made by the festival types, and videos were played on a huge projector so that the selected invitees could get a sense of the current curator's personal vision for the event. At one program launch, international guests and local stalwarts of the scene, from bestsellers to poets, as well as a diversity of races and creeds, were proudly displayed through the projectors' beaming lights, and the presentation of the program ended in a generous applause, during which we stormed out in protest. We regrouped on the walkway outside and condemned the organisers as conservative cowards for refusing to include in their highlight reel the short commercial we had shot for the festival. Though they later assured us via email that the video was to be made available on their website, this only further demonstrated how duplicitous the organisation was, by showing that they were willing to exploit the radical excitement of our subversive work, but only by doing so in a way that sheltered their privileged constituents from coming into contact with the sharp, discomfiting edges of our subversive art.

On the afternoon of our event at that year's festival, I came in early to survey the parade of wealthy, white, middle-class types traipsing across the walkways between the venues – the silver-haired women in their ostentatious necklaces and pastel-coloured dresses with their bejowled husbands whose soft, floppy faces seemed oblivious to the great machinery of exploitation and oppression that underpinned the culture industry they were supporting with their bourgeois whims and sensibilities. At the mouth of the old shipyard doors along the wharf, chairs were placed around speakers which broadcast the inane blather of some hack novelist or moralising journo. The emerald waters churned in the grey day's breezy heat, and the Harbour Bridge squatted over the event like a monolithic signifier of the nation's complicity. A volunteer in a yellow jacket and lanyard stepped in front of me when I came towards the Green Room, and I felt the coiling spring of a righteous anger ready to release itself at the thought that this drone was about to prevent me from entering the sanctuary on the assumption, no doubt, that I didn't look the part of an author.

'Excuse me, sir,' he began with a strange smile on his face. 'How long ago did you buy those jeans?' Taken aback, I was forced to concede that the jeans were new. He reached down, pinched something stuck to my right leg and peeled off the size-index sticker I'd neglected to remove before leaving the house that morning. I thanked him, and turned around to see if anyone else had witnessed this interaction, but the crowds on the wharf were busy holding hands and strolling obliviously from one festival distraction to the next, and so I went into the Green Room with a pale expression on my face, sat on a couch next to the author of a bestselling novel with a cat on the cover, who was chatting with a young poet from Melbourne whose head was shaved, and I watched from there the tiny forms of climbers in red shirts moving over the Bridge's spine, inch by inch. I started thinking about my dad, and all the time I'd spent thinking about Centrepoint Tower. I wondered if anyone ever looked at the Bridge and thought about their family; their fathers, mothers, sons or daughters. I hadn't spoken to my father in almost a year – we'd had a falling out over my evolving politics. I listened to the conversations all around, and each and every one of them seemed so friendly. There was love in the room, and I realised I hadn't been in a room like that for a long time. Outside, I saw the light dipping behind the curvature of steel above the Bridge, the sky was awash with violet cloud and the walkers in red were raising their arms up to the heavens.

Looking back on that afternoon and all that led to it from the safety of my house on Mt Pritchard, staring into the same view I had conjured up in the dim halls of the Bankstown theatre, I wonder if I've paid for my time in the cult of Western Sydney. When I was excommunicated from the group, it was discovered that I was – and had been all along – a racist white supremacist, who conspired to steal government funding from other members of the collective, and in doing so had ruthlessly exploited the hard labour of socio-economically disadvantaged ethnics in the Western Sydney region. So severe was my denunciation, it remains unsafe for me – to this day – to attend panels or readings in Western Sydney, where the threat of being passively and aggressively snubbed looms above me like an inflatable sword of Damocles. It doesn't matter: like many former cult members, I'm grateful to have my ties cut. It was fun for a little while, submitting my decency and humanity to a self-righteous cause, but somewhere between that last reading at the writers' festival and my official addition to the collective's long list of enemies, I'd come to see the fervid ideological ramblings of our movement for what they were – just another cult of personality preying on the credulity and tenderness of artistic types in need of something to make them whole – a predatory vulnerability common to those who are driven to create, and one easily exploited for amusement by a culture industry that thrives on the freak show and the carnivalesque.

IN THE ROOM WITH GERALD MURNANE

You academic types sure know how to make a simple thing complicated.

GERALD MURNANE, GOROKE, DECEMBER 2017

At a recent and highly irregular literary conference, a silver-haired professor explained that he had come to acquire his reputation by making of books 'what others had made of religion'. The conference at which the silver-haired professor made this utterance was unusual for a number of reasons – the most obvious being that it was taking place at a small golf club in rural Victoria, and that Gerald Murnane was working the bar. Adding to the strangeness of Murnane's presence, within the boxed confines of the club's bar, was the fact that the author's work was the central subject of the event's presentations. Each academic who stood behind the Rotary Club lectern to give their talk would have to handle the intense activity of the author, busying himself in the background with the club's ledger, cleaning glasses, and helping the ladies in the kitchen prepare the scones and jam.

Gerald, as attendees adjusted to calling the author, attempted to ease the tension of the situation by having the convener, another professor from Sydney, read the following announcement before the event's commencement:

Gerald Murnane wishes to inform you that he will be available to listen to some of the papers today, but he does not feel obliged to be present for all the presentations, and may come and go at varying intervals. He would like it to be known that he is licensed to serve alcoholic and non-alcoholic drinks, and that the bar will be open for both from 12 noon onwards, with the bar's licence permitting service until midnight. Anyone wishing to purchase an alcoholic drink will be required to sign the club's ledger located on the bar. While there, Gerald would like to invite you to read a three-thousand-word palindrome that he has composed, located on the opposite side of the bar.

With the tension in the atmosphere of the room thus eased for the assembled fifty or so conference attendees (the golf club's maximum occupancy being somewhere close to this number), a series of talks began on the many intricacies of an author whose reputation was such that he had managed to draw at least those fifty pilgrims from every corner of the country to a town four hours' drive from the nearest major airport.

The night before the conference I slept in a cabin outside a hotel in a neighbouring village, best known for its sizeable rock, and ate a parmigiana larger than the plate on which it was served. At the table with me were three academics who had just arrived from Sydney and Perth, respectively. One of them, a lecturer from Sydney University who had met

Murnane once before, claimed that the ecological structures beneath Murnane's writing were largely influenced by an early religious education, despite the implied author's assertion in the works themselves that this aspect of his mental imagery had long ago lapsed into a kind of incidental apprehension. By the end of our meals, as the bistro filled with families and the barking from the high-ceilinged bar began to grow intrusive to our chatter, we discovered that all four of us were Catholics of various degrees of practice, though we each went to our cabins without further comment on this coincidence.

Towards the end of the conference, a bearded academic with an American accent pointed out that most critical responses to Murnane's latest (and rumoured final) publication, *Border Districts*, had missed the obvious connection between its opening paragraph and the opening of *The Plains*, the author's most canonical work.

> Two months ago, when I first arrived in this township just short of the border, I resolved to guard my eyes, and I could not think of going on with this piece of writing unless I were to explain how I came by that odd expression.

This opening pledge to explain a resolution, the bearded academic with the American accent pointed out, is unmistakably a self-reference to the opening lines of *The Plains*, but with the essential difference that the latter begins with the narrator resolving to 'keep [his] eyes open', rather than guarded. The opening of *Border Districts*, the bearded academic argued, was in a sense a revision of *The Plains*, and this implied that, despite the author's insistence that there had been no overarching intent behind the trajectory of his works, there might be an inexhaustible form of intention at work in his oeuvre, retrospectively repurposing the themes and images of the earlier books.

Well before hearing this complex analysis, I had decided my own presence at the conference was an error of judgement. For one thing, I'd taken the place of an academic who'd dropped out late in the proceedings, and had subsequently supplied my name as an interested party. The academic who'd dropped out was aware of several books by Murnane stacked in a pile by my bedside, but what the academic did not know was that the earmarks and annotations in the books she had observed rarely progressed all the way from cover to cover. Efficiency is not my forte as a reader – I am cursed with the inability to finish the books wherein I find the greatest pleasure. The writing I most enjoy tends to get me so exercised by its effects that I am soon deep in a fugue state of mind, a kind of dissociative wandering from which I am required to return before I can come back to the page which started me off in the first place. No sooner have I read a sentence or two of this stimulating prose, which seems to awaken some novelty of consciousness in me, than I find that I have spent the afternoon hours pacing back and forth about the house, the book which started the whole thing in motion having been long abandoned on a bench in the hallway.

In academic circles this does not count as an acceptable defence for canonical negligence, which is no small failing to be sure. Among the Styrofoam and scones, one attendee asked another the name of Murnane's favourite racehorse, and the filly's name rolled off her tongue in response, no hesitation. Another asked me if I'd seen 'the church' while driving through town.

'What church?' I asked.

'Isn't that your copy of *Border Districts*?' she asked me, pointing to an uncorrected proof I'd been clutching through the afternoon. 'The one in the book,' she said, somewhat unnecessarily.

There's nothing superior about a critic who does not know their material, and there's no excuse for professional readers whose memories for fiction are faulty, but I'd hoped my usual need to plaster over lapses in attention would be less laborious in the company of readers who'd come together to celebrate the work of a writer whose implied author freely admits a failure to 'follow plots and comprehend the motives of characters' in the novels he'd read, a trait he once again asserts in the early pages of *Border Districts*, and one which endeared the author to me for all eternity when I first came across it in *Barley Patch*, where the narrator justifies his own haphazard textual memory by explaining that 'a person who claims to remember having read one or another book is seldom able to quote from memory even one sentence from the text. What the person probably remembers is part of the experience of having read the book: part of what happened in his or her mind during the hours while the book was being read.' For the narrator of Murnane's latest work, the 'image-world' of his 'inner seeing' during the act of reading is 'often only slightly connected with the text in front of my eyes; anyone privy to my seeming-sights might have supposed I was reading some barely recognisable variant of the text, a sort of apocrypha of the published work.' Doubly so, Murnane's narrator explains, when it comes to the texts and books that intend to explain the inner workings of 'the mind' through ego, id and archetype. To these 'drab' attempts to understand the mental plane, Murnane's narrator responds that he suspects his own mental territories must surely be 'paradise by comparison.'

When the bearded academic with the American accent asked my thoughts on the work from which I've quoted above, I could only respond that Murnane's writing seemed to me an extension of lapsed religious liturgy – though it was hard to explain what I meant by that.

On the drive home from the conference, I passed through a flurry of migrating butterflies erupting from the yellow grasses by the roadside. While their white bodies burst against the windscreen like puffs of chalk I realised that I could not give even a partial account of the ecstatic sense of Murnane's writing, as it seems to me, without beginning somewhere else altogether.

Many months ago, before I had the good sense to scrub myself clean of all social media, I came upon a post by an apprentice writer who was already well-known in local literary circles. Like all digital media the post was a complex arrangement of coloured pixels populated by a root logic of zeros and ones. I admit to knowing almost nothing about this esoteric relationship of numbers and colours, or the process by which they are transmitted over networks of copper or fibre optics – in this instance, the divisions of the zeros and ones and their transmission over the vast networks of cables and ethereal waves assembled on the small screen of my smartphone, in the form of thin black letters grouped into words, which were themselves ordered by an unseen intelligence abiding, from a distance, by the rules of our universal language, as dictated by the English strain of its external expression. These English words were transposed within a space beneath a square indicating the so-called 'profile' area of meaning on the electronic page, within which was displayed an image of a digital photograph of the apprentice writer's face. The transmitted display of this photograph-image appeared to have been captured outside, originally, in the golden light of a warm afternoon, and the qualities of the subject's beauty were evident even within the limitations of the square at the uppermost corner of the borders of my little screen. She appeared to be caught in a moment of joy – her mouth open and her bronze skin bathed in the gold-rust glow of the afternoon's fall.

The square in which her image was contained was arranged next to a rectangular border of apposite meaning, itself an arrangement in relation to a series of similarly boxed arenas of formal order, all of them containing their own transmissions of words and images through the electric alchemy of esoteric zeros and ones. In the rectangle adjacent to the image of the apprentice writer's face, indicating a kind of authorship over the nearby properties, the following observation was transmitted in tiny black letters within the rectangular confines displayed on my little screen: 'Writers obsess with writers, and thereby forgo an ever more interesting world.' Beneath this transmission, according, as I surmised, to a three-digit number displayed inside a box within the rectangle containing the words quoted above, were several hundred similar rectangles, all currently invisible, containing what promised to be transmissions of messages sent in response to the first message. These rectangles of response were not visible on my little screen because the logic of the system was designed for maximum usability, and so in order to make these ancillary message rectangles appear, I would be required to touch with my fingertip a small arrangement of zeros and ones depicting an arrow lodged beneath the three-digit number displayed in the corner of the rectangle containing the original remark, at which the arenas of meaning displayed on my little screen would rearrange their complex borders so that several screen-lengths containing transmissions of similar rectangles in a dialogical proximity to each other would instantaneously appear underneath the original rectangle, with transmissions of faces in boxes beside the replies in keeping with the formal authorial indices with which the first message was likewise associated.

For reasons which I could not at the time of encountering this transmission explain, reading the message about 'writers obsessed with writers', in a rectangular display bordered beside a box containing an image of an apprentice writer caught in the fine golden light of an afternoon experiencing a moment of apparently unselfconscious joy displayed on the digital slate of my little screen, caused in me a kind of psychic distress, an intense eruption of angst. Many months after encountering this transmission, I now suspect I know what it was that caused such a strong emotional reaction to what might, to the next person, seem no more than an innocent observation on the condition of writing and writers in relation to the wider world. It is not easy, however, to translate my suspicion about my reaction, except that the internal upheaval I experienced on reading the transmission about writers' obsessions and the world at large is one related to a deep internal circuitry in me associated with the concept of blasphemy – an encounter with something ontologically profane despite its intent – though I would not have been able to conceive of it as such at the time.

Even now, after many months of reflection, I am not sure how to articulate the relationship between blasphemy and the idea of literature without providing another earlier experience of the sort of dread that I now consider the result of encountering what I then understood to be unholy profanity. In a bookshop in Newtown, seven years since I'd left the inner city to live in the outer suburbs, I stepped into a bright, orderly shop called 'Better Read Than Dead' to see what books were being promoted by the staff who worked there. I had visited this clean, narrow shop with its calm blue-green storefront many times before during the years when I lived in the inner west. Always I entered the store with the same intention: to learn the opinions of the store's staff on the particular books they were at that time promoting, and to check those opinions with my own response to the first few lines of those books. Learning the opinions of the store's staff on the books being promoted involved no direct human intercourse, something that would have rendered me mute with anxiety – it was, rather, a simple matter of reading the handwritten reviews that the staff members had signed and placed beneath the books on the promotional shelves. In the same bookcase, above the books the staff had read and reviewed were the books that had sold well that week, with numbered squares on top of the shelves indicating which books had sold the best, with the number (1) indicating the biggest seller of the week's big sellers, and the number (10) indicating the lowest. On the occasion I entered this bookshop, many years after having left the inner city for the outer suburbs, I picked from these shelves a book containing a compendium of short stories written by students enrolled in the University of Technology Sydney's creative writing department. The collection was titled *The UTS Writers' Anthology*. I cannot now remember whether this book was located on the bestseller shelf, or whether I was opening it to compare my own reaction to its contents with the account written and lodged beneath the book by the store's staff.

In the opening pages of the book I found an introduction by a writer who was at the time very popular, and who had recently won several awards for her latest work, though, as I'm sitting in the outer suburbs writing this account, I cannot recall either her name or the name of her award-winning collection. At the end of her introduction, most of which I have forgotten, the following remark was printed on the rough recycled paper of the anthology: 'Reading fiction is perhaps one of the few remaining secular paths to transcendence – that elusive state in which the distance between self and universe shrinks, long symbolised in literature and philosophy by a blue flower.'

Reading these words some years after I left the inner city for the outer suburbs, where I am now writing this account, I can recall a vague sense of the sickening looseness I experienced, in the distance between myself and the rough recycled page on that particular afternoon in the narrow bookshop; a kind of motion sickness in the still confines before the borders of its neat teal shelves. Such was the intensity of the feeling that it seemed as if I had to reach a long way to put the book back in its place. I felt as though I might lose my footing in the reach. It is by no means obvious to me now, reflecting on the words by which this reaction was provoked, where precisely, in those thin lines printed upon the rough page, the source of that disorienting shock might be located, but I recall that I felt, vaguely, at the time, that the author of those words about the blue flower had taken some mental image of a sacred doorway between one world and another, and had pressed it between the pages of her introduction, so that an impression of its diffused essence had lifted from the materiality of the page and wounded my sense of reality, stranded as I was, momentarily, between the world of the page and the real world.

Sitting in my old house on the hill in the western suburbs, in the heat of a twenty-first-century summer, with the rotating fan shaking the wilted leaves of the pot plants by the back door, I cannot recall how I dealt with my encounter with the words about the blue flower, written in the collection I discovered in the narrow confines of the Newtown bookshop many years ago. When I run through the many clipped reels of memories linked to the mental image of the narrow store and the words on the page and the cyan shelves, in search of lost time, all my attempts to follow the reader I once was, as he retreats from the book he has placed back upon the shelf, begin to unravel. I see him, thinner and fuller of hair, as he passes beyond the glass doors of the store, and the mental projection of what that afternoon might have looked like, leaps up and turns the memory to fiction, a scene assembled from cinematic clichés, of a slow rising-away from the busy pedestrian parade of Newtown's streets, the parapets of shops built beyond living memory, and the reader who I once was, lost in the bright crowd forever passing along King Street, into the train station and the cafés, the hotels and bazaars.

Far easier, less fictional to recall, is my own reaction to the more recent encounter with the social media message I began this odd digression by addressing. I had come upon this transmission as I was sitting on the couch in the lounge-room, and as the distress provoked by the post about 'writers obsessing about writers' flooded my being, I leapt from the couch, tossed the offending phone into the cushions, and fled to the bedroom, where I sought sanctuary behind the always-closed blinds, to consider the 'ever more interesting world' the young author had described. I hazarded a peek between the blinds of my dark little room, and took the time to examine the unlettered streets of my mountain town atop the outskirts of our city, in which – both city and room – I had spent the majority of my life, except for some brief and foolish sojourns in the east.

Through the blinds the street was satisfactorily uninteresting. Directly outside the window a curved strip of road ran sharply across the top of our molehill suburb. For many years the curve of the road meant that it was customary for me to wake in the night to a sound not unlike an explosion just outside my window, to pull open the blinds in half-wakefulness and observe cars overturned in a wreck of broken wire fences and savaged tree trunks, the halos of headlights pointing directly into the windows of our house, the wheels still slowly spinning in the darkness as someone crawled out of the twisted door of the car onto sheets of broken glass, their limping figure disappearing into the night while the neighbours turned on their porch lights and waited in their pyjamas and singlets for the police and tow-trucks to come and clear the air with their blue and red lights and their searching torches.

The street I observed through the blinds after reading the comment from the young writer on social media contained no such drama. It was a mild afternoon in September, and I observed only a few features of that familiar territory: the hood of a white Hyundai parked on the lawn coroneted with jacaranda blooms, thick oleander stems lurching in the breeze with their knotted brown heads out of flower, and beyond them the sepulchral grey and brown concrete slabs of homes that inner-city critics would call McMansions, with spiked steel gates and fences around their borders like barbican defences extending to the edge of the curb. Passing through this suburban scenery was an ancient man on a motorised chair, rolling down the sloped curve of the road with what seemed to me a demented abandonment to speed, the little red flag fluttering atop the bending antenna on the back of his vehicle, his long red socks standing high on his corrugated calves.

Having observed nothing in particular of interest through the window, apart from the old man on his motorised chair, I felt reconciled to the impression that there was something mistaken about the claim I had read by the young author, that the world outside words, the so-called real world, was perpetually increasing in its degree of interestingness. The absence of interesting elements outside permitted me to give a nervous shrug to no one, and to turn my attention to the stunted walls of books that I had stacked about my room. I looked at the covers and assorted shapes of the novels and collections assembled and stacked into strange totems about the room, which I had been unwilling to see when I entered, as though to look at them with troubling associations in my mind before checking on the outside world would introduce an uncomfortable impurity into their materials, which it might later be difficult or impossible for me to expunge.

The piles of books are like the stones placed at the points of a septagram star, warding evil from the borders of my bed. In the dust of childhood, in the room where I slept in the bunk beneath my younger brother, watching the springs of his mattress tick and clink as he moved fitfully in the night, I lay awake in an insomniac's decade-long pervigilium, retreating from sleep to escape the night-terror paralysis that plagued my bed times, fretful always of my mother's teaching that a stray devil crept about the house in the dark, and could strangle us in our sleep were we to lose our wits.

Sleeplessness was my defence against this in-between world of sleep and terror, inhabited as it was by the threat of opportunistic demons. As any hyper-insomniac can attest, the upper limits of long-time exhaustion are also peopled by diabolical figures – shadow men most common of all, appearing in the deprived vision at the periphery of sight in those who reject rest. Otherworldly phenomena also accrue in weeks without sleep – walls slant and rotate, lights begin to gesticulate, stars seen from the window seem to move at the will of mental command, sounds increase their sharpness among other oddities of misapprehended experience. The strangest of all was the sense that would impress itself upon me at the height of all exhaustion, a feeling of great emotional presence accompanied by the sensation that what was uniting all things, in some unspeakable dreadfulness, was a structure of immense proportions balanced delicately upon the most fragile spindles, like a great castle seen from the sky, thick at its towers and thin along its walls, suspended sideways in an infinitude of empty space. The feeling this image provoked ran simultaneously through my fingers and throat and wrung such heavy tears from my eyes as to leave me sobbing in the sheets.

When Kafka writes, 'It is not alertness but self-oblivion that is the precondition to writing,' I suspect I understand what he means. When I first began to read, which is itself a kind of writing, it was to escape the immense wasteland of sleeplessness. There were no smartphones or tablet devices to numb the disorientations of the mind then, and so I turned to the forgiveness of my stepfather's book collection. Fantasy, for the most part, made up the supply – each novel more alike than the last: an elf, a dwarf, a man with a sword and a romance subplot. One series, whose name I have long since forgotten, followed a band of wizard-folk who waged a guerrilla war to save their lands from an evil sorcerer. For the most part, they camped out in the forest and cooked skinned rabbits over an open fire, and made stews in pots with salted meats, while the bearded old wizard argued with his witch-wife, their bickering inevitably ending with the wizard sighing and saying, 'Yes, dear,' as the companions smirked knowingly. For a child of a broken home, who had no reason to disbelieve the scripture teachers when they said that we would not see our parents in heaven if they failed to uphold the sanctity of marriage, these fictional marital disputes were a torturous distraction.

On these endless nights with the strange rectangular device of the paperback pressed into the pillow, and my body bent over it like some ascetic yogi frozen in meditative prayer, I traced the thin shapes of the letters on the page and felt the images of the novel's story running through my mind like a film, while I edited these images into a secondary story, on the fly; one in which I inserted myself into the narrative and changed its destiny. At the campsites, with the rabbits roasting on their ad hoc spits, I'd enter from the dark of the woods, a powerful wizard myself, and admonish the magical married couple for their petty bickering, 'The world is at war!' I'd screech at them both with a booming voice, eyes glowering with a great wizard's potency, 'Can't you see your real enemy is out there – not here between you!'

When the writer of this series of novels, the title of which I have long ago forgotten, eventually revealed that he had co-written the books with his wife, adding her name to the cover of all subsequent releases, I felt an enormous sense of betrayal. All this time, the marital tensions of these magical characters had been a surrogate for the supposedly real relationship of the author and his wife. It had all been a fake, a meaningless device! To discover such cheap self-insertions passed off as genuine fantasy disgusted this young reader, and I turned my back forever on the kind of fiction that Murnane calls 'film-script fiction', that vein of fiction that is solely aimed at creating in the mind of its readers a certain series of imaginary scenes. It was a sin, I decided, to bear false witness, even in a world of pure imagination.

All of this, these unimportant eccentricities of an early readership, I would never have allowed myself to remember were it not for the work of Gerald Murnane and the permission that his acclaim grants to all that he has deemed to record in his volumes. When the narrator of Munane's *Barley Patch* recalls a mystery novel called *Brat Farrar* that he read as a child, and the images of its green paddocks and part of a homestead shaded by trees, he recalls that he likewise felt 'as though I moved among the characters'. Though he could not, as I had done in my own interjections into the world of fantasy, alter the events of the novels he read, he was 'free to take advantage of the seeming gaps in the narrative'. The 'unreported whole days, months, years even', which are conventionally skipped in any given novel, were open territory for Murnane's narrator to occupy at will with a version of himself, free to 'observe and admire' the landscapes those fictions offered.

The narrator of *Border Districts*, as the bearded academic with the American accent would likely have noticed in his reading of the book, expands on this image of a narrator reading a version of himself into the novels he encounters – this time with the narrator not remembering the experience directly, but rather imagining a man who is remembering himself as a young reader. The portrait supplied by the narrator is of a man who recalls that, from an early age, he began to experience the snatches of fiction he glimpsed in the many novels his parents left by their bedside, as parts of a never-ending book made up from apparently disparate fictions. The books his parents borrowed from the local shopping-centre library were all connected to the one imaginative space, 'a far-reaching landscape of pale-green meadows interspersed with patches of dark-green woodland'.

Each meadow was bordered with flowering hedgerows. In each woodland were paths leading past banks overgrown by wildflowers with appealing names. Here and there in the landscape were large houses of two or more storeys and with numerous chimneys. Each house was surrounded by a spacious formal garden at the far end of which was a park with an ornamental lake. Each large house was occupied for the time being, not only by several of the latest generations of the family that had owned the house for several centuries, but also by a floating population of youngish men and women who were distant relatives of the owners of the house, or who had been recommended to the owners by some or another friend of a distant relative, in a city that might have been named London and was no more than a conjectured smoky blur far away past the furthest of the pale-green meadows.

Despite the various and differing populations of this ever-present landscape, the man the narrator of *Border Districts* imagines to be remembering his youthful reading can recall only two figures: 'a young male character and a young female character'. Anyone else has been forgotten.

These 'reports' of a narrator who imagines a man who recalls the dimensions of fiction are themselves not fictions – the narrator of *Border Districts* insists that we are reading an account of 'seemingly fictional matters' rather than a formal fiction per se. The narrator assures his readers of this in the context of failing to remember a quote from Proust 'purporting to explain why the bond between reader and fictional character is closer than any bond between flesh-and-blood persons'. Unable to uncover the quotation from his files, the narrator offers us his own explanation: 'sometimes, while reading a work of fiction, I seem to have knowledge of what it would be to have knowledge of the essence of some or another personality.'

Murnane's narrator seems in the above passages of *Border Districts* to argue for a profound truthfulness in fiction, but also places the narration itself outside fiction's confines, and so it is somewhat unclear if the truthfulness of fiction through a series of 'seeming knowledge' is also claimed by Murnane's own work.

The conference in the golf club in rural Victoria ended with an address from Gerald Murnane titled 'The Still-Breathing Author', in which he described himself as a 'technical writer'. Although Murnane is a pedantic grammarian, it is not clear to me in what sense his work is 'technical', and the author's own explanation of this label, 'I mean by this that my work as a writer is to search for the sentences that will most accurately describe the mental imagery that is my only available subject-matter', seems perversely idiosyncratic. Whether or not the reader believes the narrator of *Border Districts* that his work is about 'seemingly fictional matters', there is no doubt that the ideal of an essential truth is central to an understanding of the author's work. As evidence for this, there is the author's own assertion that it was Jack Kerouac who gave him the technical capacity to move from being a reader of grand internal landscapes to an author of such spaces. Here is Murnane, in an essay from *Invisible Yet Enduring Lilacs*, describing his first encounter with *On the Road*:

> The book was like a blow to the head that wipes out all memory of the recent past. For six months after I first read it I could hardly remember the person I had been beforehand.
>
> For six months I believed I had all the space I needed. My own personal space, a fit setting for whatever I wanted to do, was all around me wherever I looked...my space coincided at last with the place that was called the real world. But the world was much wider than most people suspected. I saw this because I saw as the author of *On the Road* saw. Other people saw the same streets of the same Melbourne that had always surrounded them. I saw the surfaces of those streets cracking open and broad avenues rising to view. Other people saw the same maps of Australia or America. I saw the coloured pages swelling like flower buds and new, blank maps unfolding like petals.

Is it mere coincidence that it was Kerouac, the most Catholic of Great American Writers, whose ecstatic landscapes opened the imaginative plains to Murnane? Kerouac himself suffered deeply from an authorial uncertainty until he deigned that his duty towards writing was to tell, directly, the truth as he lived it. It was some conception of the Truth that drove Kerouac to write his novel about 'Two Catholic buddies in search of God' in *On the Road*, based on his experiences traversing America in the forties. It is the characteristically ornate aesthetic of Catholicism that permeates the work of both these great writers, an aesthetic that is in essence an attempt to express the experience of an infinite, divine creativity present in the material world. Both Murnane and Kerouac attempt in their works to distil the unfathomable depths of finite matter through an ecstasy of revelation and praise.

In its logic this aesthetic is compatible with the pantheist conception of the world that Murnane aligned himself with in his talk at the end of the conference in the golf club in rural Victoria. Where Kerouac was ecstatically open to the passionate embrace of everything and everyone, the great 'IT' of a Dionysian Christ – punctuated by depths of confessional sorrow and suffering – Murnane's passionate witnessing is, as *Border Districts* begins by attesting, performed with saint-like constraint. While *On the Road* ends with a climactic bacchanalian orgy in a Mexican bordello, the jukebox playing so loud that the walls shake and the actors are drenched in sweat, the crescendos of *Border Districts*, by contrast, are purer, peripheral discoveries of surprising interconnectedness. In one of the most intensely focused accumulations in the book, Murnane manages to connect a marble, an eye, a book cover and a kaleidoscope with a ray of light – pinning these elements together with such gathered emotional intensity that its sudden culmination in a series of names of colours verges on an imagistic symphony. The minute dimensions of these ordinary objects are explored with such tenacious and elemental prose that the relational significance they bring together, pierced by a ray of light, is an expression of their interconnectedness on a complex transcendental plane. The narrator who witnesses this act of relational significance is the curator of the guarded eye, the mystic who can gather the heralding of apparently meaningless parts into an infinite whole.

This climax with its purity of colours, '*Crimson lake, burnt umber, ultramarine...deep cadmium, geranium lake, imperial purple, parchment...*', is immediately followed by a transition in the narrative, into a long discussion of the link between patterns of colour and the specificity of particular moods. Certain shades of red, forgotten, represent, so the narrator of *Border Districts* tells us, a loss of whole associations in memory and experience. It is in this passage too that we learn that our narrator has long understood maturity as something to do with conforming to boundaries, however arbitrary. He tells us how, as a child, he had sought to impress his elders by conceiving of certain parts of his immediate environment as categorically out of bounds. Soon the narrative breaks again, and the narrator tells us he has just returned to his writing after spending some time in the city. The journey from the city to the border town is itself a temptation of associations – the narrator, failing to guard his eye, is caught up in an immense digression of connectedness: images related to landscape are dislocated by street signs, and these ensnare him in an unsolicited chain of thoughts, leading to the recitation of the names and heraldry of racing families and their various geographical connections, structured in a manner reminiscent of certain biblical genealogical lists. It is only another return, to the calm purity of colour, which is able to interrupt this propagation of uninvited associations: the narrative flow of these thoughts is soothed by the narrator's admiration for 'any person who could rely on a single colour or shade to represent him and his family'. It is this simplicity and purity which holds the narrator in thrall.

> I knew something of heraldry. I had studied in colour plates in books numerous images of coats-of-arms. But none of these complex patterns had affected me as did the assertion by some or another so-called aristocrat that he needed no chevron or fess nor any quarterings of gules or vert or argent; that he challenged any inquirer into the nuances and subtleties of his character or his preferences or his history to read those matters from a jacket and a pair of sleeves and a cap of defiant simplicity.

In part the pleasure this purity gives to the narrator is the thought that he might himself one day 'light upon one or another shade or hue that would declare to the world as much I cared to declare of my own invisible attributes.'

It is this principled pleasure in purity and simplicity which divides the Catholic Kerouac from the 'technical' Murnane. Kerouac – who drank himself to death at the age of 47, whose final work was perhaps the longest suicide note ever published, who could not live the life he affirmed in his work – believed he found God on his travels. Murnane, by contrast, when asked at the conference by the silver-haired professor how it was that he had poured so much imagery into the plains and yet they remained largely empty, explained his conception of his inner imaginary in terms not unlike these: 'Within a house on the plains, there is a man downstairs in a large room reading a book that is part of a long series of books. A woman is there too, and she is reading the same series, but she is reading so intently that she has not noticed the man's arrival.'

'How's that for an answer?' Murnane says to the professor.

At the conference, a young biographer discussed the pleasures of being given access to Murnane's famous archives, and in a recent essay, this same young biographer wondered how it could be that his subject had garnered so little acknowledgement from the literary establishment in the form of awards and titles. Was there, the young biographer suggested, some conspiracy of refusal behind the neglect Murnane had suffered through his career? I suspect the truth is that there is something essential to the work itself that repels the threat of acknowledgement by any award or honour. When some or another guru called Kerouac 'The Christ from Duluoz', the author called it blasphemy, and it was in this moment that the title for the beat writer's final, fatal novel *The Vanity of Duluoz* was born.

The conference, with its pilgrims and their words of praise, was the culmination of a writerly life lived in faith. *Border Districts*, beginning with a resolution to keep faith, ends in strict observance of this tenet. The narrator, explaining a distaste for the poet Shelley as 'fatuous and affected', explains that he nonetheless 'foresaw, soon after I had begun to write this report, that I would be compelled to include in it a certain two lines from some or another poem by Shelley: lines that I had once found merely decorative and without meaning but have remembered for more than fifty years in spite of myself'. Murnane's narrator supplies the lines, one poet quoting another, as Kerouac insisted Christ became on the cross when he quoted a Psalm of David 'like a poet remembering it by heart'.

The sun set over the flat sandy greens of the golf course as Murnane's lower lip quivered and he thanked the speakers for their words, and spoke of the spirit that had kept him writing when he thought nothing on earth could compel him to continue. There was a strange change in the air, and the author admitted to feeling it too: 'I didn't expect you to win me over today...and basically you have.' With that he retreated to the confines of the bar, to a round of applause, and for an hour or so, sold drinks and signed books. I stepped into the queue to buy a Carlton Draught with a copy of *A Million Windows*, and overheard a critic with a shaved head say, 'I wonder if we will one day understand what we have here, in this man.'

## Acknowledgements

In earlier versions, several essays in this collection, or extracts from them, have been published in the following publications: *Sydney Review of Books*, *Meanjin*, *Seizure*, *The Lifted Brow*, *Global Media Journal* and *Sonofabook*. Thank you to the editors – especially Catriona Menzies-Pike, Jonathan Green, Alice Grundy and Ellena Savage.

The collection is the result of the superlative work of the indefatigable Ivor Indyk, Evelyn Juers, Nick Tapper, Léa Antigny, Emily Stewart and Aleesha Paz.

Thanks also to those writing friends whose lunacy and bizarre behaviour was a constant source of inspiration – especially Fiona Wright, Felicity Castagna, Lachlan Brown, Hugh Newton, Ian Van Gemert, David Henley, Milissa Deitz, Melinda Jewell and Rachel Morley.

Final thanks to my family for all their love, support and chardonnay.

The Giramondo Publishing Company acknowledges the support of Western Sydney University in the implementation of its book publishing program.

This project has been assisted by the Commonwealth Government through the Australia Council, its arts funding and advisory body.